After The
MORNING CALM:

Reflections of
Korean Adoptees

After The MORNING CALM:

Reflections of Korean Adoptees

Sook Wilkinson, Ph.D.
and
Nancy Fox

Editors

SUNRISE VENTURES
708 Parkman Drive
Bloomfield Hills, MI 48304

ISBN: 0-8187-0286-9
Library of Congress Control Number: 2002232787

ATTENTION NON-PROFIT ORGANIZATIONS, AGENCIES, COLLEGES AND UNIVERSITIES: Quantity discounts are available on bulk purchases of this book for educational purposes or fund raising.

For information, please contact SunriseVentures@hotmail.com.

Printed in the United States
Harlo Printing Company
50 Victor, Detroit, MI 48203

This book, a labor of love, is dedicated to my niece and nephew, Chelsea and Forrest, adopted from Korea by Kelly and Stephen Wilkinson.

Sook

To the thousands of adoptees with whom I have worked, it has been a privilege to participate in your lives and especially meaningful with my children through adoption, Tony, Kari, Betsy and Irina.

Nancy

Contents

Foreword

Reading the stories in this book concerning different issues of being adopted gave me a sense of enlightenment. There were many stories I could relate to. For example, I related a lot to **Mirrors** by Kara Carlisle. Not knowing where you fit in because you feel Caucasian for the most part and then you look in the mirror and see a whole different person. That has always been an issue in my life.

I also related to **Carefully Taught** written by Christine Jones Regan. When I was younger and even still today, people say racial slurs. I had a similar childhood growing up in an Italian based home. You grow and get to know that culture, but on the other hand, you are so curious about your own. It is hard for parents who are not familiar with the culture of their child's origin themselves to try and teach it to their adopted child.

A story in particular also gave me a sense of hope. Having wondered if my birth mother ever thinks of me, the thought has sometimes lingered in my mind. Mary Lee Vance in **To be of**

Credit states that in almost all cases, the birth mothers of adopted children admit to never having forgotten the child who had been placed for adoption. For some reason, that gives me almost a sense of relief.

It amazed me to know and read how similar many of us are. It makes me feel relieved that I am not the only one. It was like I made friends without even meeting these people.

Stephanie Lagman,
18 Years Old, Korean Adoptee

Acknowledgments

We thank all the contributors who courageously told their stories. A special acknowledgment goes to Dominic Pangborn who titled the book and designed the cover. The center picture of the cover is from his birthplace taken on his last trip to Korea, the Land of the MORNING CALM.

We thank our Advisory Committee members, Hyun Sook Han, Amy Harp, Martin Kohn, Dani Meier, Ph.D., Joyce Pavao, Ph.D., and Chris Winston for their valuable advice, wisdom, encouragement, comments and editing. Gail Berkove, Ph.D. and Stephanie Lagman also contributed through careful review of the manuscripts.

We thank Mike Hathaway, Joanne Kabat-Hyzak, and Vicki Lansky who so willingly shared their expertise in the publishing world.

We thank KAAN Newsletter, Jan Adler, Suzanne Ehlen, Teri Bell, Becky McLennan, Alyssa Martina and the staff at Harlo Printing for their help in more ways than they may realize.

We thank Todd and Jon for their loving patience, support, and faith in us.

We thank our friends, colleagues, children and other family members for being there when we needed them the most.

INTRODUCTION

Sook Wilkinson, Ph.D. and Nancy Fox

The idea for this book of anthology began about 3 years ago. With the 50th anniversary of international adoption of Korean children approaching, we wanted to honor and celebrate all those who navigated their new lives abroad. Contributors were solicited by using the electronic technology of various list serves and KAAN Newsletters. Out of those who responded from the U.S.A., European countries, Korea, and Australia, we selected 26 stories to feature. They are in the form of poetry, essays, and letters.

Acknowledgment is given to the contribution the previous publications, specifically _Seeds from the Silent Tree_ and _Voices from Another Place,_ made to the direction of this book. This book, **_After the MORNING CALM_**, builds on their strengths and voices. What sets this book apart is that it is edited for adolescents and young adults as well as all others related to the adoption community.

The editors, in their professional experiences, have observed that many adoption-related questions and issues surface as the children enter into adolescence and young adulthood along with their increased cognitive and emotional capacities. Often, many wrestle with them silently and alone. The contributors tell compelling stories from their heart pertaining to embracing their multiple identities, overcoming adversities, searching for birth parents, making their first return visit to Korea, and giving back to their communities, among others.

The first Gathering of Korean adoptees in 1999 in Washington, DC also impacted the formation of this book. Men and women who ranged in age from late teens to 50's shared how the issues of transracial and cross-cultural adoption related to their lives. Many of the core issues of identity, birth and adoptive families, grief and loss discussed at the Gathering are well represented in the book.

The integrity of each written piece is respected by delivering the stories in the contributors' own words. No one said it better than this 9 year old:

I hold in my hand
the key to my heart
which no one knows how I feel.
I open the door with the key
and then I feel all better.

Ian Frederik, Korean adoptee

We feel honored and privileged to have come to know these wonderful people who have so generously shared their experiences, wisdom, pain and joy.

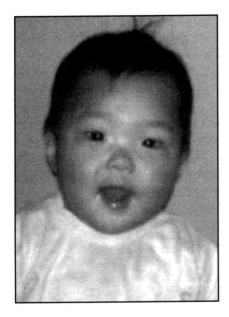

Kara Carlisle
karashae@hotmail.com

Kara, 24, — Mo, In Ae – is a 3rd year student completing her Masters of Divinity. Adopted at age 5 1/2 months old, she grew up with an adopted Korean sibling. Her passion lies in writing, traveling and education (Feminist, Multicultural Studies, Liberation Pedagogies, Community Education). She made her first trip to Korea in 2000 at age 22, then again in 2001 to meet her extended birth family. While she grapples with how to approach old-new relationships, she truly feels grateful for the healing that her reunification has initiated in her life and in the lives of many here and across the globe.

Mirrors

Kara Carlisle

I have been "white" for most of my life. Until about three years ago, I was most comfortable with that identity; it was the only way I knew how to be. It was only when I looked in the mirror that I was reminded of my difference. You see, my family, friends, church, school—all were White American. The only Korean I really knew was my adopted brother—whose identity is also culturally rooted in White America. For me (since I cannot speak for my brother), the impulses to explore the image in the mirror would intermittently come and go—usually overpowered by the relentless call to "fit in" and at a deeper, more painful level, by the voice whispering to me, "You will *never* fit in." So, I went about my business avoiding mirrors and trying to forget the face that looked back at me.

Almost two years ago, something happened. A friend was snapping photos and I offhandedly said—"I hate getting my picture taken." To which he tenderly replied, "Whoa, that is really sad. What's going on there?" I paused, unexpectedly struck with emotion. "What *was* going on?" I began to ask myself. Later, as I stood in front of the mirror, I wept. Hurt and ashamed, I tried to really *look* at myself. Painfully and desperately, I stared. Whose face is this? Who do I look like . . . anyone? Where do I fit? Dear God, will I ever belong? So, with my indistinguishable Korean face and my distinctive American heart, I climbed into bed that day and eventually fell asleep.

For most people little time is spent thinking about from where they have come and like whom they resemble. They have their father's nose, their mother's curly hair, and somehow ended up with their grandfather's crooked teeth. And the perpetual question "Who am I?" does not leave any one of us alone for very long. Even in these most basic and superficial observations an adoptee is haunted.

Most adoptees grow up looking like no one. For Korean adoptees, we rarely even *resemble* anyone. Most Korean adoptees to the US grew up in the Midwest, in white American families and with little exposure to other cultures or racial groups. I was no different. So a month ago, when I visited Seoul, South Korea (the place of my birth) and came face to face with my birth father, my past, and myself, I was overwhelmed.

For the first time, I was not a random face, disconnected from Korea and not so conspicuously "white." I was not only Kara Shae Carlisle from Indiana; I was now Mo, In Ae from Korea. The face in the mirror that had been a source of confusion and a reminder of my elusive past, suddenly found its place alongside the broken man, my birth father, in front of me. It was during that meeting that I realized that it was not only I who had been afraid to look at the face in the mirror.

We shared stories, tears and confessions that day. We shared kimchi, subway seats and the same brown eyes. We share multiple identities, a painful past, and the hope of things to come.

It is difficult to express the significance of such a meeting; I am sure I do not yet know it myself. I am realizing, however, that I must not be afraid to look in the mirror. I can no longer deny the parts of me that cause pain—somehow trying to convince myself that the questions will go away. I cannot escape my past, nor do I really want to. Instead, I must keep staring at the reflection in the mirror.

I am more Korean these days than I have ever been. The paradox of Brown and White swirled together, the confident American and the orphaned Korean, Kara Shae and In Ae . . . I do not know if I will ever "fit in," per se, and that is okay (I wonder who *does*).

I do know that these days, when I pass by a mirror, catching my reflection, I don't turn away so quickly. I wonder . . . when was the last time you looked into the mirror?

Dominic Pangborn
Dominic@pangborndesign.com

Dominic, the President and CEO of Pangborn Design, is a highly recognized and successful graphic designer and painter with a strong belief in giving back to his community. He has contributed tangibly to many cultural and community organizations in the Detroit area through his art and business. More importantly, he gives generously of himself. His avocation is to "love people from all walks of life." His passion lies in traveling and meeting new people to build bonds, to be a mentor, and to be inspirational. He designed the cover of this book and gave it its title.

19

Love the Life You Have

Dominic Pangborn

I was 10 years old when I, Jung Sun Hun, said farewell to my mother, my brothers, my sister and to Korea. My mother was a Korean villager and my father, an American soldier, who I never met. I was a mix of Korean and Caucasian physical features. Although my fellow villagers accepted me, I faced intolerance and bigotry from many outsiders.

My mother was concerned about the troubles I might face in Korean provincial life as a mixed-raced child and decided that America would be the best option for me. She approached an American missionary who was visiting our village and explained my situation to him. She asked if he could take me to the United States. The missionary agreed to help.

I lived temporarily with an elderly woman until my adoption could be arranged. Many Koreans suffered great losses in the Korean War and this woman was no different. She lost her husband and child in the North. However, she was unable to carry on with her life and her bitterness ran deep.

She expressed her anger and rage through daily bouts of verbal and physical abuse. I was unable to see my mother except for a few days when I could sneak away and we could spend time together without anyone seeing or recognizing us. As time passed, I worried that my journey to America would never happen.

Luckily, the missionaries came through on their word. They worked through the Korean and American legal systems and arranged for me to move to the United States. I said my good-byes and was put on an airplane for the very first time.

I was adopted by the Pangborn family in Jackson, Michigan, and was renamed Dominic Joseph Pangborn. I was a middle child in a family of 12 children and I did not know a word of English or much about American culture. For the first week, I did not understand that the other children in the house were my new siblings. I assumed they were the neighborhood children who had come over to play. When they didn't leave, I thought I was living in an American orphanage.

The Pangborn family accepted me as one of their own which eased my transition. I eventually overcame the language and cultural barriers. However, at the same time, I lost touch with my Korean roots. My Korean family and I lacked the means to contact each other. We had no idea how the other was doing or even if we were still alive. This lack of communication would continue through the years to come.

As Dominic Pangborn, I grew up like any other American kid, playing football, attending dances, and hanging out with my friends. After high school I moved to Chicago to pursue a career in art. After graduating from the Chicago Academy of Fine Arts, I returned to Michigan to stake my claim.

In 1979 I founded Pangborn Design, Ltd. in Detroit. Through lots of hard work and dedication, it became one of the most recognized and well-received successful graphic design firms in the city. Grateful for my success, I chose to give back to the community. I serve on many boards in the Metropolitan Detroit area which promote the arts, medical care, and cultural diversity.

Despite my professional successes, I felt incomplete not knowing what happened to my Korean family. I had had no contact with them since 1962. I decided to find them to let them know that everything turned out wonderfully for me. More importantly, I wanted to find my mother who had given me the strength and inspiration to go forward. I knew the difficulties she must have faced rearing a child of mixed race. What courage she must have had, to be proud of me and care for me more than her other children. What pain she must have endured to give me up not knowing whether we would ever see each other again.

In the early 1980's I returned to Korea. Although I did not remember much of the language, the Korean culture and customs came back as fresh as when I originally left. With an English-speaking university student as my guide, I found my way back to my small farming village. The countryside had not changed much since I left. Nearly every detail of the country was how I remembered it.

I eagerly anticipated the reunion with my family, but upon returning to the village, I was greeted with the tragic news that my mother had died a decade earlier. I never, never expected to return to the village only to find my mother gone. I was prepared for her sickness and poverty but not for her death. It was a moment I will never forget.

I argued that they were wrong and hoped that they were referring to someone else. I stood in silence with tears pouring and the world around me became silent. In a short time, the sun fell behind the clouds and everything was gray. There were no colors in the faces of the people, none in their clothes or in the landscape. Then the rain fell and no one moved.

Slowly the elderly woman who brought the news of my mother took my hand and we walked in the rain to her grave. I stood there for 30 minutes while everyone watched from a distance. With a saddened heart, I paid my final respects to her, fully appreciating all the sacrifices she made on my behalf.

As I was leaving the village, an old man approached me. At first I did not recognize him but then realized he was my childhood friend's father. He remembered me and gave me a letter that my brother had written to him from Seoul over five years ago. He was not sure if my brother was still at the same address but it was a good start. The next morning we got on the train to Seoul.

We found the address. It was a steel factory in Seoul where my brother worked. My guide and I approached the security gate asking about my brother's whereabouts. The security guard went inside and a short time later, the supervisor came out to inform us that it was my brother's day off and he would guide us to his house.

I saw a group of children playing in the yard. One child looked up at me and paused before running inside. Moments later, a face appeared in the doorway — and both of our eyes teared in disbelief. We embraced — something we had not done in 20 years. As soon as my other brother and sister heard of my return, they all came over with their families.

I realized how lucky I am. Not everyone has the love of family and friends. For me, I am fortunate to have two families, one in my father's land and the other in my mother's land. I keep regular contact with my Korean siblings and their families. I have made several visits back to Korea and they have visited me in the United States.

I also remain very close to my parents in the United States and my American siblings. My wife and I are very proud of our son who is now running his own company in Chicago.

My life experiences in Korea and the United States have taught me this:

Love the life we have. Life is precious and we should not be concerned about the "Whys and Hows" we came to be. With love and caring, do all you can with life for yourself and for others.

펴 화

pyeng-hwa

Mi Ok Bruining
skidding@hotmail.com

Mi Ok, aka Song Mi Ok, aka Anne Mi Ok Bruining, 41, is currently a poet, writer, artist, activist, international adoption consultant and future art teacher. Living in Cambridge, Massachusetts, her interest lies in bicycling, horses, film, photography and travel. Education includes an MSW in Clinical Social Work. Adopted at 5 years old into a family where she is the only adoptee and Korean, her birth family consists of a mother, two brothers and extended family. Mi Ok has also lived and worked in Korea from 1996 to 1998 and plans on visiting Korea on a yearly basis.

Can a Tiger Climb Trees?

Mi Ok Song Bruining

One year ago
today,
I arrived here
to Korea.

The orange-colored trees
were decaying.
The river was muddy
& stagnant,
& the mountain became too steep
to climb.

I returned
after twelve long years
of running away
& running towards the yellow ghosts—-
to plant my own tree,
forge a new river,
& climb up a different mountain.

Autumn—-

I chopped down the trees,
drained the river,
fell down the mountain—-

& returned
to the ancient & sorrowful soil
where I had been conceived.

Would I find what I was looking for?
Would I be found by someone
who was looking for me?

Winter—-

I became a displaced parcel—-
a product of my birth father's rage

towards his stunted & twisted trees,
& his failure to conquer the slippery mountain
while he drowned in the shallow river.

Now, today, one year later—-
I have found
what I was looking for
& I was found by someone
who was looking for me.

Spring—-

Learning about
my birth mother's own bare trees,
parched rivers
& barren mountains,

I now know the aching truth
of her own sorrows
in not being able
to grow her own trees,
cross rivers & climb mountains
with her only daughter.

I know now, that I was sent away
to greener trees, cooler rivers,
& higher mountains.

Summer—-

I love & hate this country—-
for her majestic trees,
looming mountains
& icy rivers.

I have seen the yellow ghosts,
high up in the trees—
with the tiger
by the river
at the foot of the mountain.

As a foreigner, I am asked
what are the trees I can call my own,
how do I swim in the rivers,
& where are the mountains I climb?

Autumn—-

As an outsider, I am naming
my own trees.
I am discovering
my own river,

to claim my own
mountain,
plant my own trees
& calling the yellow ghosts
home.

I am the tiger
crossing the river
& climbing up the orange-colored tree
for a better view
of the yellow ghosts
on the mountain.

Seoul, Korea

Kathleen Ja Sook Bergquist, Ph.D.
klbergq@ilstu.edu

Kathleen, 40, is an Assistant Professor of Social Work at Illinois State University. Conducting research and writing on topics of transracial adoption and cultural competence are particular professional interests to her. Kathleen was adopted at the age of 20 months from Seoul. She is the mother of two bi-racial birth sons and Brittany Soo-Jin, adopted at the age of 3, from Taegu, Korea. "As an academic I write a lot about adoption, but never about my own personal experience. I was motivated to write this piece more for my daughter than myself; it's my attempt to capture our paralleled/intertwined experiences."

Let It Flow . . .

Kathleen Bergquist, Ph.D.

Some say blood is thicker than water; I say love is thicker than blood.
>   Senator Paull Shin,
>   Korean adoptee, 1999

. . down the Han River . . . through our veins . . . spanning generations . . . across oceans . . . joining stories . . . hearts and lives.

The cabin exhaled a sigh of stagnant transpacific air into the jetway as the last of the passengers disappeared into the concourse. Most of the passengers were already in the terminal hugging their arrival party or anxiously searching for their connecting gates. My eyes scanned the doublewide 747 and rested on a mop of black hair bouncing down a row of seats and a cautious eye appearing around the headrest of the last seat. A leery glance and Soo Jin made her way back down the row with the energy only a

34

three year old could muster after a 14-hour flight.

Ja Sook's distant starved eyes landed briefly on the face of the cooing visitor, quickly returning to the disintegrating butter cookie in her small grip. Nestled in a large strong lap, she need only focus on not letting go of her prized possession. Preparing the passengers for final descent, the flight attendant continued down the aisle, smiling and reminding weary travelers to fasten their seat belts and return their seats to their locked and upright position.

Korea, from this day forward, for better or for worse, in sickness or in health, is relegated to being a picture in an adoption album, a place one reads about in glossy picture books, or sees in documentaries on PBS. We were given a one-way ticket.

After being "christened" with the ceremonial first bath and wearing brand new a-little-too-snug-because-mommy-didn't-realize-what-a-big-girl-you-were pink baby doll pajamas and bunny slippers, Soo Jin pours over a child's book about Korea. I join her on the floor, pointing out the hanbok, taegukki, and kimchi as she chatters in toddler Hangul and impatiently turns the pages.

Her excitement or agitation, I'm not sure which, seems to increase as she continues and she starts to kick her chubby legs against the floor of the hotel room while the volume and pitch of the chatter escalates. As if in utter exaspera-

35

tion, Soo Jin flails the open pages of the book with her slipper giving it a bunny beating as she admonishes the pictures.

Language . . . I don't have the language to understand what she is saying or the words to explain to her why she has been taken away from everything and everyone she knows. Soo Jin quietly sings herself to sleep with children songs which are dancing around in her head. I imagine her voice being lifted and echoed by her playmates at the White Lily Orphanage and am haunted by the solitude of her solo.

A formidable Hawaiian blue shirt with white plumeria flowers and thick sun-leathered farmer's arms gingerly embrace Ja Sook, this American haroboji's newest granddaughter. As she pressed her diminutive body against his expansive chest and curled her head under his square German chin he strolled away for a private discourse with his newly arrived gift from Korea. They both fell in love that day . . . Ja Sook and grandpa.

"Omma" rings through the house and out onto the street, as if being funneled through a sieve, followed by doors slamming with a shudder and determined feet careening through the hallway. To this day I am transported whenever I hear the sing-song cry of a Korean child clamoring for omma's attention. Brittany Soo-Jin appears with her forehead knotted, as serious as a doctor prepping a surgical team, with tales of indiscretions her brothers have committed to herself and mankind.

Eyes down, as if contemplating her unsteady legs, Kathleen Leilani Ja Sook is anchored to the floor of the lanai. Lost within a body limited by neglect, she purveys the world with a solemnity borne out of deprivation as a hobby-horse-riding Korean Roy Rogers encircles and gallops off into the living room in pursuit of more responsive foes. A molded plastic hug from a golden haired doll is thrust upon Kathleen by her onnee wanting to play. Bewildered and uncertain Kathleen startles into tears as the unfamiliar engulfs her.

Her theatrics rise to standing ovation caliber whenever a camera lens is leveled on her. Unabashedly Brittany Soo-Jin takes center stage and launches into a flirtatious diatribe with an off-camera accomplice. Between performances . . . she escapes into another world surrounded by playmates to whom she whispers almost inaudibly. I wonder if she speaks to onnee and obba, I will never know . . . as her language and memories unceremoniously slip away . . .

Surrounded by an orchestra of pots and pans and armed with a wooden spoon, Kathleen Leilani listens for the rhythms of the Pacific Ocean with the concentration of a conductor, arms poised mid-air. Siblings' voices waft through the kitchen on a wave and mommy smiles "Hello Kathy" as she breezes through with an armful of fresh laundry. Kathleen gathers her first hesitant smile for her new omma and they begin the journey of learning to be mother and daughter

"Soo Jin-ah!" Brittany snaps her head

around as if to extinguish my voice and with a "Please, not in public" roll of the eyes. Hesitantly she heads toward me, her shiny black pony tail bouncing as she plods along, digging her heels into each measured step. Her left hand flies to her hip as if to stop it as her head tilts in a sideways glance. I extend her favorite pink sweater for her to slip into and she lingers just long enough to get one arm in, running away as she pulls the other side up over her shoulder.

Kathleen could feel her heart climbing out of her chest as she and Mark race to point out things to each other, the squawking cry of parrots throwing colorful feathers at the crowds and the pungent odor of captive monkeys scaling their cages. Mark spotted the familiar roundness of an East Asian face amidst the more angular animated faces of the local Hindi and he proclaimed with a mischievous smile, "Look Kathy. He looks like you!" Kathy noted that the man bore a striking resemblance to her brother despite his protestations, with his fair complexion and wiry Asian hair . . . but chose to not point out the obvious, and lunged after Mark with a retaliatory smack that barely brushed him as he disappeared into the crowd.

Before the air could suck the heavy metal framed door shut, I heard a smoke strangled voice say, "You look just like your mama . . ." and I smiled. Brittany leaned against the carry-out counter as she took the bait. "Yeah, you think so? Everybody tells me that," as she reels the unsuspecting woman in. She fixes her eyes down, running the tip of her shoe along the edges of a grease-stained tile. After listening to an assessment of our genetic similarities, Brittany counters, "Well, that's interesting considering we're not biologically related," slowly raising her eyes to register the response.

Walking thickly through the chalet foyer, numb from the slopes, we headed toward the bank of elevators anxious to get out of our damp clothes. Like a row of ducklings following too close, we bumped into each other as Dad stopped too abruptly. Seated in front of a well-fed fireplace, a booming voice flagged my father down with the over-familiar manner Americans have with each other when in a 'foreign' country.

Greetings were exchanged as his glance panned over us and his hooded eyes narrowed on Mark and me. He asked incredulously, "Where did you get them?" Blood rose like mercury in the noon-day sun as my face burned with horror and shame. Mutely I screamed at my Dad to keep moving. I watched unbelieving, like a silent movie. I saw their lips move but the words were lost spinning above my head and my eyes were burning with a water-fall of tears frozen by their pleasantries.

I burst through the door with the dramatic entrance of a prepubescent teen and buried my sobs in the white duvet of my parents' bed as humiliation and embarrassment poured out of me. I explained through wet stutters that 'that man' talked about Mark and me as if we were things . . . disposable souvenirs . . . something that had been bought and paid for.

Helpless, my father paced furtively, running his fingers through his hair as if massaging his scalp, searching for an appropriate response. Halted by inspiration, he reached into his shirt pocket and withdrew 'that man's' business card and symbolically shredded it into the wastebasket.

I sat transfixed in front of the television as Deann Borshay's disquietly intriguing adoption story drew me in. Intermittently I would entreat Brittany to join me, my voice wandering down the hallway and muffled by her resolutely closed door. After a sustained stage pause she emerged only to pass through the living room. Like a passerby at a gruesome car accident, she tentatively stole glances, not wanting to appear overly interested. She nodded fleeting acknowledgments to my commentary and quickly retreated.

Our stories are the same, interchangeable, yet unique and they are the blood that flows between us, mother to daughter, adoptee to adoptee. She sees herself in me as I do her, yet she has a Korean mother and I don't . . . but love flows from my adoptive mother through me to Brittany. It's the love that sustains us, and the Han River that flows through our veins that joins us. Yes, love is thicker than blood . . . but we must be able to share the power of the Han with our children so that they may understand their legacy.

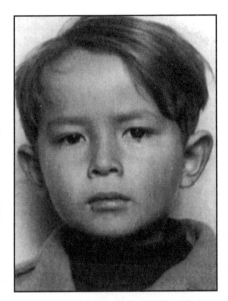

Thomas Park Clement
mectralabs@mectralabs.com

Thomas, 50, nicknamed "Alien," adopted at age 7, is the President and CEO of Mectra Laboratories, a worldwide distributor and manufacturer of medical devices. He has received many awards in his lifetime including Distinguished Alumnus Award from Purdue University and Role Model Award for Inspirational Work in North Korea from AKA (Also Known As). His essay, "A Journey into the Past," is from one of his many humanitarian mission trips to North Korea. He is a member of Advisory Council on Unification, appointed by South Korean President Kim, Dae Jung. His avocation and passion are his community service and all things related to Korean adoptees worldwide.

A Journey into the Past

Thomas Park Clement

After watching CNN and seeing the condition of North Korea due to the three years of flooding, I decided to travel on a medical/famine mission to North Korea. There were reports that over two million have perished from disease and starvation related to the flooding.

Being in the medical business for almost 15 years, I've made some excellent contacts with presidents of other medical companies who, with no hesitation, responded to my request for medical donations for the mission. Mectra, the company I founded, acquired approximately $73,000 in supplies which we delivered in March of 1999 through the help of the Eugene Bell Foundation. The EBF has been on many missions to North Korea to help fight TB. When I was in Korea in the 50's, I was treated for TB by a similar organization.

There are several reasons why I picked North Korea for my mission. The primary one is that

North Korea is comprised of Koreans. It is the last artificially divided country left on earth. The people have a real need for exactly what my company manufactures — surgical equipment used in laparoscopic surgery. Having been orphaned, I know hunger and disease. I did not realize that the trip for me would be visiting the "ghost of Christmas past."

Our guides met us at Pyongyang airport. We had brought many boxes of devices and medicines which were all x-rayed prior to leaving for the Koryo Hotel. The hotel and the rest of the city looked pretty much like any other city with subtle differences. There were no traffic lights. Instead, policemen and women directed traffic at major intersections. The streets were much wider than in the US, more like the streets of Beijing.

Humor does not translate well into other languages. It was a relief that our guides had a wonderful sense of humor and we became fast friends. During one of our trips, a shock absorber on the car broke on the side that a fairly tall and heavy Caucasian doctor was sitting. The driver and guide were laughing and said he broke the shock because he eats too much. At a restaurant, they laughed when I made a face at a snake that was soaking in some sort of liquid. They wanted me to try it although they knew I would not. On other occasions, we drank beer and talked, giving me the impression that people are practically the same the world over.

The rest of the EBF delegation left me in

Pyongyang for three days while they traveled north to visit some TB clinics. During this time, I lectured at the Pyongyang University Medical Center where the donations were delivered.

The experience of being left behind was the first ghost I encountered. I have experienced being airlifted into another society where I did not speak the language before. I now began to feel unnerved again in Pyongyang. When I was adopted in the U.S., my orphanage information indicated to my soon-to-be adoptive parents that, "Little Tommy does not baby talk." After boarding the airplane headed for the U.S., in 24 hours, I could no longer understand anyone and no one in America could understand me.

Here I was in the DPRK with the same problem but in reverse. I could not speak Korean and the Koreans with me could not speak English but my new friend, Mr. Kang, made me feel at ease. He took me sightseeing to various beautiful locations around the city. We went bowling and played ping-pong and pool. We talked about many different aspects of life and its' hardships and the devastation created by floods and famine. Nevertheless, three days later when I met up with the rest of the delegation, I was relieved.

We traveled from Pyongyang to Wonsan, which is on the eastern coastline. Most visitors are not allowed to leave the hotel without an escort but we were allowed to travel because we were visiting various rural TB clinics and hospitals. The highways were not asphalt and had been greatly damaged by the flooding. The road over the mountains was gravel and it hugged the steep mountainsides as it curved around every ravine.

The few vehicles we saw were large army vehicles carrying soldiers to and from work sights. This was the second ghost. In America and abroad, you usually don't see that large of a military presence. I had not seen this, or the long lines of people on foot, since the Korean War.

The realization that these people were Korean brought back the most vivid memories of my past. I had witnessed the shelling during the Korean War, the wounded, the smell of firearms and had witnessed the devastation war brings. I remember walking along roads in Korea with a throng of migrating wounded. Being in the presence of so many army personnel brought the war back to me.

From Wonsan, we traveled straight north for about seven hours to another coastal resort where we visited more hospitals. It was there that I saw my third and final ghost. We had all met in the lobby of the hotel to walk down the street to the restaurant together. Just outside the doorway, a small homeless boy about five-years-old was standing barefoot next to the step.

He would not make eye contact and just stood as we passed. The proper etiquette for us was not to stop and make an incident. He was my protégé. He could have been me. I could have been that boy. His image lingered with me the rest of the trip.

I have to question how in the world I got from there to here? What strange chain of events occurred in my past that I could travel such an immense distance? I've gone from where he is now to training surgeons.

It finally all made sense to me. Seemingly meaningless pieces of the puzzle all fit together. The purpose of this whole exercise was to help each other. I would not be there if it were not for the help of those who had the insight, the pioneering insight, to bring me through life's travels.

My life has been filled with irony. On a previous trip, I had met President Kim Dae-jung. Imagine a beggar child meeting a president and telling him not to worry about the past! So, I have walked the poorest streets of Korea and have walked the halls of the presidential palace.

I am a war child yet have returned to my motherland to help both the South and the North. I am an inventor with two dozen US patents and I am the president/CEO of a medical company whose devices have literally touched the lives of millions of people.

If my life had a message, it would be that every child needs to have love and be loved by a family. I am half Korean and half American. Orphans must have an equal chance to excel in life, just like anyone else. We need equal rights in EVERY aspect.

Adoptees today are articulate, well educated, high-tech, organized via the web, and have a global virtual community to be admired. We are constantly working on improving our world community. Our lives are a living symbol of the inherent goodness in human kind. God bless.

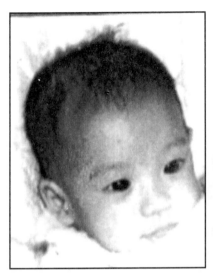

Christine Jones Regan
Regan317@earthlink.net

Her Korean name, Suh Yun Hee, means "Face of an Angel." Christine, 29, hopes that her essay will provide validation for young people who might be experiencing struggles for acceptance and identity. She works with women and children as an advocate. Her story is dedicated to her mother, who recently passed away after 14 years of brave fight against cancer, and her loving father. Christine and her husband, Brian, are new parents to a beautiful daughter, Aisling. This essay was first published in Bamboo Girl, #8, January 1999 issue.

Carefully Taught

Christine Jones Regan

Recently an employee of mine suggests that I take a look at the new photo-essay book entitled <u>TWINS.</u> At first, I am puzzled. I am not a twin, nor do I have any siblings. I have met the twins who had compiled the photos and biographies in the course of my occupation and my initial assumption is that this must be the reason I am being asked to check the book out. However, as I flip through the pages, I stumble upon a set of Korean twin sisters adopted by Americans, more specifically, Irish and Italian Americans. Now it is becoming clear...

Their biography describes the now grown women's struggles through the years as each tries to gain her own independent identity. As I read on, I compare similarities to my own life. Then I see what is intended for me. In the first paragraph, one twin describes a day in grammar school. While discussing family heritage, she declares that she is Irish and Italian – to which the teacher promptly corrects her, telling her that she is not. Confused, the young girl cries – and at that moment, so do I. It is a circumstance I remember all too well.

I was born not too far from Seoul, Korea and was found shortly thereafter in a police booth, waiting to be rescued. At the tender age of 14 months – tiny and helpless, I was greeted by two very anxious new parents, a new extended family, and the photographer from the *New York Daily News*. "Two Korean Tots Land in a New World of Love" the centerfold's headline boldly declared. I had finally arrived.

Back in those days, prospective adoptive parents adopting a child from another ethnic background were simply instructed to "love it" no different than any other biological child. My adoptive parents, both Irish-American, believed this wholeheartedly and were armed with much enthusiasm. The Joneses were ready to shower me with all the love and affection they had. The *New York Daily News* was partially right; I had landed in the *New World* of Brooklyn, NY – a home certainly filled with love. Later I would learn that the outside world was not so sweet.

My adoptive mother, the only mother I have ever known and the only one who has ever mattered to me, likes to tell two stories. The first is about how she spent many of the early months trying to lull me to sleep each night in my crib, always to no avail. One day a co-worker tells my aunt that Korean orphanage babies do not sleep in cribs. They sleep on mats on the floor and that the crib most likely scared me to death. That was one problem solved and some well-deserved rest for both mom and dad.

The second story is about the day that my mother fed me a cookie, which quickly crumbled into tiny bits in my playpen. She watched as I meticulously picked up each and every crumb from the floor of the playpen and my pajamas, eating each morsel as if it were my last – despite the fact that the much larger piece remained in my other hand. It was then that she understood the blessings we tend to take for granted: those of warmth, food and shelter. She cried.

As the only minority child growing up in a predominantly Irish and Italian American neighborhood, I soon discovered that I was not the same as the other kids on my block. Initially the differences were less noticeable and the slights minor. However, that would change rapidly after my family moved to the bigger home in suburban New Jersey. I was still a minority but now one in an even less diverse town.

The irony was that my parents chose to move because they believed I would benefit from a safer environment and better educational opportunities. In the eyes of my parents, I was no different than them or any other child with whom they could have been blessed. Our home was filled with affection, caring and lots of TLC. At home, my adoption was explained from an early age and became a natural part of my vocabulary and my life.

In contrast, the *education* that I rapidly received when I stepped out my door was one that taught me that I was different and alien to my classmates. I was a "gook," a "chink," a "boat person" and a "V.C." (Viet Cong). My actual origin was not important enough to know. Conversely, to teachers, clergy and my own extended family, I was "adorable," a.k.a. "a little china doll."

In the schoolyard, I was ridiculed and taunted, picked on and beaten up. I was pushed in the mud, chased and threatened with sharp objects, had my locker vandalized and pages from textbooks ripped up and plastered with such phrases as, "Go Home, V.C." or "You killed my uncle in Vietnam." For an entire year in Catholic school, I ran from a boy who screamed in my ear, "Pork Fried Rice," with the perceived stereotypical *Asian accent*. I was so deeply bothered by slurs about rice and chopsticks that I never wanted to be seen eating anything as such. Likewise with karate and kung fu, I would not agree to take karate lessons as my mother had wanted for my own protection.

Some girls in my high school ordered me to "get down on all fours and bark like the dog that I was" and I refused. Later they physically beat me and I finally was able to convince my mother to allow me to leave school. But it was almost too late. I felt invalidated and silenced. It was

53

not until I became an adult that I was able to come to terms with my parents regarding those painful years.

As an impressionable child, I was led to believe that I was unworthy of companionship by the opposite sex. As a young adult, this theory changed slightly. I became desirable, but not worthy of a *real* or *public* relationship for fear of what friends and parents would think. I felt as though I was never good enough and obviously never better than my *white* classmates.

The fact that my parents were Caucasian allowed for some forms of acceptance but not much. I was not good in sports and I was smart but then, "All Asians are like that anyway, right?" Growing up without any understanding about my own Korean heritage left me with an extremely damaged self-esteem.

I know my parents' naiveté was not intentional. They believed that they could love and raise me as their own and they tried hard as hell to do just that. Unfortunately, the simple logistical needs of food and proper bedding were really the basics in what should have been a much more thorough primer into the finer points of raising a *multicultural* child.

As an adult, I now value and cherish the relationship I have with my parents. My heart holds an enormous amount of gratitude for the wonderful opportunities they opened up to me. I am adamant when I say that at no time do I believe that adoption itself was the issue. The real issue was and still is about education and cultural awareness. I still believe in adoption, yes – even interracial. However, I find myself urging new adoptive parents and those considering this step to examine their own values about race.

I want to say to them, "Take stock of yourselves and your reasons for adoption before bringing a new child home." It is unfair and ultimately harmful to deny that prejudice and bias exist or to assume that love will conquer all. Love is strong but there are realities that must be faced.

Children need to have a sense of pride in their own heritage. They should be allowed to celebrate as many cultural activities as they so choose – and only if and when they freely choose. I have every right to embrace my Irish-American heritage today and my Korean heritage tomorrow, without question or ridicule. This is the right of every multicultural person.

Dealing with the multitude of prejudices that befell Asian women and me in particular, it would have been beneficial to have had strong Asian role models. In some ways I am still seeking them. What might these role models have shown me? What would I want to know if I had a chance to live my adolescent life again?

I wish I had been warned about how some people would feel compelled to ask me uncomfortable questions about my American surname, about my heritage and about my adoption. I wish someone had told me how much it would hurt to be rejected by the families of men I was interested in, and sometimes the men themselves, simply because of my race.

Maybe I would have been safer if I knew how to deal with the advances of men who believed that Asian women were toys of subservience. Or, about the employers who feel that they can ignore the contributions of Asian women. If only I knew to expect *that* reaction, that incredulous look on the faces of people meeting me for the first time after talking to me on the phone – and assuming I was Caucasian. Most of all, I wish I was told that I was beautiful because of all my Asian features.

Many of my experiences might seem to echo those of a number of non-adopted Asians, since we are still being treated as somewhat "invisible" in many areas. However, I speak here for future adoptees. Lacking a support system from others who truly understand cultural differences, the adopted children's coping mechanisms may not be as strong. They will have – just as we now have — much to offer society. It's time we **are** heard.

This is not THE END of my story. It is only the beginning.

Yang Kwi Hwa, aka Eileen Thompson-Isaacs, EThomps451@aol.com

Kwi Hwa, a Korean/Filipino woman, was adopted at age 18 months in the late 1950's. Her interest in the effects of race, culture and other facets of identity development has been the impetus for much of her personal and professional life. She is an advisor for the Big Brother/Big Sister program of Tufts University Korean Student Association. Through this program, Korean adoptees and their families are matched with the Tufts students for a cultural connection. Currently, she works at Wheelock College Student Counseling Center and lives in the Boston area with her husband and two children.

Alphabet Soup

Yang Kwi Hwa

i have no story
i have no words for the story
i have no true beginning
i have no imagined end

i am the story
i live the story
the words escape from my story
and become a jumble of alphabet soup
in a language I don't recognize

i am in and out of focus
so odd that I can help others
find words for their stories
but not for my own

Peter Kearly
pkearly@hfcc.net

    Peter, 30, was known as Kim Ki-Hyun when he was adopted from an orphanage at the age of four. He had an academic scholarship to Wayne State University where he obtained a Masters in Arts and is currently completing his Ph.D. in English literature. As full-time English instructor at Henry Ford Community College, Peter is incorporating his strong belief in helping people of diverse backgrounds understand each other better through writing and reading literature.

I'm Iwish

Peter Kearly

That's what I couldn't seem to get through to Ms. Goodman. Of all the other kindergarten children, shouldn't she have listened to the only one who was absolutely sure about who he was? Sure, my tongue didn't yet heal from having its frenum cut which I guess is a not so uncommon operation for Asian children. But my message was clear; I was "Iwish." Why else would Da make sure to point out to me that John Wayne was Irish, that the great jazz musician, Gerry Mulligan, was Irish, that the greatest author, James Joyce, was Irish. Why else would he teach me the difference between a shillelagh and a stick?

When the teacher had my parents try to explain to me what being "adopted" meant, I still couldn't understand why I couldn't be Irish. If Da said he was Irish, then I was Irish too. It didn't matter where I came from. At least it didn't matter until I became convinced that where I came from should matter, when I could no longer try to simply ignore the taunts of having a flat face, squinty eyes and buckteeth. Then the traits that I thought I shared with my dad, his self-assuredness, his athleticism, his wit and aptitude for making friends, no longer seemed related to me.

How different we were became more obvious each time we crossed the border from Windsor, Canada back to Detroit. I can't completely blame the border officials for not recognizing in me any legitimate signs of Americanness. I often look at the photograph stapled to my adoption "birth certificate" without any sense of recognition. How could my jolly face in the flesh match the distressed jaundiced face of the three year old in the photo? How can I even be sure that the birth date on the certificate is my real birth date?

Without an actual birth certificate, the orphanage had to keep some kind of record of my existence and so created a document that might serve the same purpose. I know that that document, though, hides more about my past than it shows. The circumstances of my abandonment float somewhere between what is on paper and the memories of a birth mother that I may never meet.

I try to take solace in the idea that my birth mother never left me. She appears each time I study my face in the mirror. I see her in the folds around my eyes where wrinkles will form.

I see her in the dimple in my left cheek and the mole just below my right temple. I feel her in the warm embrace of my adoptive mother, entrusted through a universal maternal agreement.

At four, actually three and a half, I was one of the oldest children on the plane from Seoul to Chicago. I have faint memories of the stench and vomit and the whines of confused and anxious infants and toddlers. For my mom, I wasn't the oldest on the plane; I was the most responsible. She loves to recount how I helped to console the other children on the plane. I wonder if I wasn't just fitting a role already established in the orphanage where the older kids were expected to help care for the younger ones. But such a fact can't dim my mother's fond memories of my arrival, memories that seem to differ inextricably from mine.

Against the radiance of hers, my memories seem less enchanting and even cynical. In fact, my mother can carefully account for my skewed memories. I had to wear a girl's blouse, for heaven's sake, and a bowtie cinched so tight she had to cut it off. She often laughs as she retraces this image of a boy made so uncomfortable by the feeble attempts of a Catholic orphanage to make its adoptees look presentable to a modern American family.

Soon after I came, Stanley, the family fox terrier, was put to sleep. My brother's brown and white furry pal became replaced with a thick black haired boy with tawny skin. My coming probably had little to do with Stanley's going. (Stanley did have a history of mental illness, I'd learn, and his brain most likely couldn't handle me constantly confusing him for a "wolf.") But several years would pass before another dog entered the house and this dog would be a gift for my sister. As a child, I would never have a dog of my own. My mistake was that I never learned the American custom to point and ask for what I wanted.

One Christmas, my brother received a science set, complete with microscope and petri dishes. Empathetic to my envy, my brother invited me to compare my hair to his under the microscope. His hair was blond and thin, barely visible; mine was coarse and black. When my mother called us over to cut our hair before we'd go to Grandma's for holiday supper, she'd taken out her sewing scissors for my brother. For me, however, she had to buy professional electric barber's clippers.

I'd watch my mother swiftly cut my brother's hair, leaning back once or twice to be sure that the bangs were straight. Then came my turn. The electric clippers would whirr and hiss clumps of bristly black hair to the floor. This Christmas, though, the whirr and hiss left steam rising from my scalp and the smell of singed hair. I pointed fervently for my mother to stop cutting. How relieved she looked when her adopted son finally learned to express what he wanted.

When I tried to express what I wanted in

grade school, however, my Asian-ness seemed to always get in the way. I began to blame my Asian-ness for my awkwardness on the playground rather than ask my parents to enroll me in any team sports. In middle school, I wanted to be popular with the girls but the only popularity I received was by way of allowing classmates to copy my homework.

I didn't want to be like the Asian geeks I saw in movies like "Sixteen Candles" and "Revenge of the Nerds." I'd watch with my lighter complexioned friends and laugh along with them. Laughing, I thought, would distance me from the popular Asian looking icons of American humor. I did not want to be another typical Asian overachiever, both praised as a model minority that other people of color should follow and denigrated as an emasculated sex-starved wallflower. I tried to stay away from the other Asian guys at school.

By my senior year in high school, I finally did manage to date some girls but never more than for a few weeks at most. I wouldn't allow myself to believe that any girls dated me for any reason other than to satisfy some curious interest in my ethnicity or to express sympathy for an Asian nerd. Even the Asian girls seemed to only date white guys. The few that passed a kind glance my way or allowed me to drive them to school would eventually be seen in the arms of a white guy. I didn't want to ask an Asian girl on a date just because she was "Asian," at least the kind of Asian female that American movies have men fantasize about. I didn't want to believe that I wanted a geisha or a dragon lady or a cute lotus blossom.

By the time I began college, the pressure to have a girlfriend subsided and the academic personality that was so awkward throughout public school finally found a niche. I learned to funnel my anxieties of the past into an anger of the present. I learned to point and say what I wanted. I began to understand that I wanted to have some control over how others view my Asian-ness. I could tell fellow college students that my academic and professional success should not overshadow the racial inequality others have experienced or continue to experience.

Now, as a college English instructor, I know to a certain extent I am valued because I know English well *and* because I am not white. Sometimes when I teach, I sense non-white students being comforted in knowing I overcame the so-called language barrier that English can create. I feel a sense of honor and duty as such an example for my students. However, I am also aware that my colleagues may see in me a source of ethnic diversity that I myself would not claim.

Not that I still desire to be Irish. I just don't want to be merely Asian or Korean, especially since I actually know very little about the peninsular nation stuck on China like a bent hangnail. I suppose despite my adoptive parents deepest desire for me to truly feel like theirs, I have inherited an illegitimacy that cannot be easily resolved. But, I don't mind being a bastard as long as I can point and say how my bastard-ness should be interpreted.

Geoffrey van Veen
geoffreyveen@hotmail.com

Geoffrey, 29, is a Dutch Korean adoptee, born in Taegu, Korea. Through Arierang, an organization for adopted Koreans in the Netherlands, he has met many other adoptees in Europe. Cooking is his passion while he works as an account manager for a company in ICT sector. This story was written when he first visited Korea and met his birth family including his father, stepmother, a sister, a half-brother, and a grandmother.

The Journey Back

Geoffrey van Veen

I said goodbye to my mother at the Schiphol Airport in Amsterdam. She cried. I cried. Our emotions found their way like a river finds its way through the landscape. Sorrow, anger, pain? Twenty years wrapped in one moment. For a brief moment I felt very connected with my mother. Mother and son, then and now, one moment. Twenty years ago and this moment, my mother and I and no one else. There we stood. The journey had begun. Twenty years ago we were there too, at the airport, then with many more future parents and many little children from far away Korea.

For three weeks, I was going to Korea to see my birth land. One and a half weeks ago, I had a call from Korea. My friend, Don, had found my family. Packed and ready to go, I stood there with my girl friend in front of the customs control.

The trip began well, I must say. The airhostesses of Korean Air are very pretty. Nothing better than traveling in good companionship. Not that they have much time for you. They have to work like hell to serve the passengers. A good conversation is also out of the question because their English is, so to say, not good. So you can only look at them and, even when you pay attention, they have to run.

It reminds me of my flight to Holland. Then we were small children and small children like to play. We played in the airplane. We ran after each other, we laughed, and we ran through the aisles. What would the other passengers have felt about us? Irritation because we disturbed their quiet flight.

After ten hours flying, Korea finally came in sight. That was about time. Although the travel time to Korea has become much shorter, ten hours are a long time what with sleeping in a chair, the air conditioning, and all the noise. It softly rained when we arrived at Kimpo Airport. When I got out, a blanket of hot air came over me like a warm welcome. For a second, there was a lump in my throat. For a brief moment, no tears, no sorrow, but a feeling of coming home.

When you come home for a holiday, there is your house, your family waiting for you. You are seeing everybody with new stories to tell. Everybody healthy, no strange things happened. You are back in your room; all your things are there, at the right place. Everything feels secure.

Of course, now this was not the case. The feeling of relief was of twenty years of waiting, the feeling that this was going to happen only once. Now the moment was there, now I had come back to Korea. I would meet my family after twenty years. That was the feeling of relief. Only it didn't feel reliable.

This country was stranger than Spain, than Italy or Mars. Here everything is upside down. I couldn't read nor understand the language. The people looked yellow and their eyes were small. This was the country from photo albums, from documentaries, far and away. Here I was alone, a stranger. I was like Jan Weltevree, the Dutch mariner, stranded on the beaches of Korea. A Dutchman in a far and unknown country, lost from God and civilization. A country that didn't exist on the map.

After the customs clearing, I met Hyon-Tek. Hyon-Tek was a good example of Korean hospitality, Korean kindness. I still have a picture of him standing with Don and me, like three brothers who have come together after a long time, happy. Hyon-Tek had studied for a year in the Netherlands and he was coming home to Korea to see his family again, just like me

In that way, we were a little bit connected here at the Kimpo Airport. But yet our lives were so different. Although we just met, Hyon-Tek already felt responsible for me. Maybe it was because he had studied in Holland and liked to see Dutch people but there was something else, something I could not explain. It was a part that was not coming from hospitality or kindness.

Later on I also found out that more Koreans had these feelings of what seemed like collective guilt. This guilt is towards adopted Koreans. To understand this, you have to understand the Korean people. Every Korean is a relative; they or we come from the same ancestors. The collective well-being of the Koreans is a responsibility of every Korean, in the past, the present, and the future. They believe it is the fault of all Koreans that so many children had been adopted abroad. In the last ten years, their views on overseas adoption have changed. A time has come to face the shame.

In Korea, I found the people, the culture, the food, and the rhythm totally different. The City of Seoul, a big city, 24/7 ongoing. To be there gave me a rush, a continuous euphoric state of mind. I was a tourist in a strange country. I had to discover everything. Behind every corner was a surprise, an adventure. Every meal, the dish was something to look forward to (except Burger King and Pizza Hut).

Our hotel room was also an adventure. We stayed in a "yogwan," a small hotel. As ordinary Westerners, I wasn't sure of what "yogwon" meant. After inquiries, the term "love hotel" popped up but is also a good shelter for budget travelers like us. Our room was very comfortable. Everything was within reach of our arms length. The king size bed only took half of the room space. I can guarantee this gives an extra dimension to your vacation so if you are not too picky, I can recommend it.

Seoul is a big city with over 10 million people. Above the city is smog which can compete with that of Athens or Mexico City. Especially in the summer, the combination of smog and the enormous humidity creates an unpleasant climate. The presence of smog is not strange if you see the traffic jams in the city. There are wide streets with taxis, buses, cars and trucks, all driving like madmen. There is something in the collective driving style of Korea that tells me the insurance rates are very high.

While I found above ground very dangerous, under the ground is much safer. There is a big network of subway lines. The subway is nice and easy transportation with regular trains that take you almost everywhere. However, like above the ground, it is very crowded even at night. But that is Seoul, day in, day out, 24 hours a day, 7 days a week, all the year through.

I cherish these memories of Korea and, now and then, I think about them. Yes, life was great and adventurous. It is better, though, not to have illusions about overseas — it was not a paradise for me. To spend my whole life in Korea is not my idea of an ideal life. Korea has too many elements that are unpleasant and unfamiliar. For me, it was good to be there and to enjoy the pleasures, to stay long enough and get the kicks. But...not for a long period. I missed my home — the Netherlands.

Kate Hers
Kate@onegook.com

Kate, 26, is a Korean American conceptual performance and visual artist. Most recently she has performed at the Midwest Ladyfest in Chicago and the Baewha Women's University Annual Fashion Show in Seoul. A graduate from the School of the Art Institute of Chicago, she received Finalist Award Illinois Arts Council and a Fulbright scholarship to Korea in 2000. She was awarded a Blakemore Foundation Language Scholarship in 2001, and taught performance art at Kaywon School of Art & Design in Seoul. "Are You Korean?" first appeared in Fulbright Review, Spring 2001 issue.

Are you Korean?

Kate Hers

I used to answer "yes" when people asked me this. Because, truly in my heart, I believed I was Korean. But later, I realized that I was answering, "yes," to a different question. Now, when a Korean asks me, "Are you Korean?," my answer is "No." I answer to *his* meaning of "Korean."

His meaning of Korean is that your parents are Korean. You would have heard Korean, at least a tiny bit, even if you cannot speak the language. You also know what Kimchi tastes like since you were young. In addition, his meaning of Korean is not that you had only a vague notion where Korea was on a map. He did not grow up with people who did not share the same skin color, same culture, same background.

For a long time, I thought that there was not just one way to be Korean. Being Korean could be very broad and diverse. However, I realized that my way of thinking was very Western, very American. Korean people feel that being Korean is unique in nature, something to be proud of, this sameness that runs throughout the blood of "my people." I say this tongue in cheek.

I now believe that this sameness of Korean people may be why Korean will never succeed in an international cosmopolitan sense. I will never entirely fit the code. Not only because I cannot walk the walk and talk the talk, but I do not feel "their" way. Some things about Koreans make them unique and entirely different from other nationalities, other races.

As an example, there are a few words in Korean that do not exist as words in other languages, such as English. Just because English lacks these words, does it mean the concept does not exist in other countries or that non-Korean people cannot understand them? I do not think so.

Han: grudge, a heartburning, rancor, spite, hatred, grief

Jung: feeling, emotion, love, affection, sentiment, passion

Gi: spirit, energy, strength, vitality, pep

Of course, the meaning of these words is much more complicated than the dictionary's translation. These words are deeply entrenched in 5,000 years of history, culture, language, and arts. I cannot assume I can completely understand the meanings in a completely Korean sense. However, I feel that we as human beings have felt similar emotions and can understand them as living beings. This is why perhaps I think that I will never truly be a Korean in the Korean sense of the word.

In Korea, being Korean is just one thing. There is no distinction between race, culture, and nationality. People do not have to explain themselves because everyone's background is similar, or at least they pretend to be. In the United States, everyone, if not faced with it on an everyday basis, is at least aware of the issues of black and white, Asian and Latino, Middle Eastern and native American Indian, etc.

Just because one's face is Asian does not mean that one is not American. Being an American means many different things. When Korean people assume that an American is white and only speaks English, I see their limitations in thinking. This is why I am not sure they will ever understand that being Korean can mean many different things to different people, just as being an American does not mean one type of person.

We, as members of the human race, are complicated and complex people. Our identity should not be limited to one type.

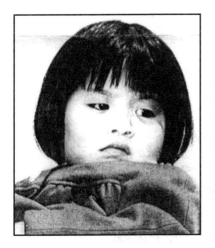 

Mary Lee Vance, Ph.D.
mvance@staff.uwsuper.edu

Mary Lee, 44, Director of Undergraduate Academic Advisement at the University of Wisconsin-Superior, is responsible for coordinating undergraduate advising initiatives. She was one of the first Korean adoptees to arrive in the States during the 1960's. Since being diagnosed with Post-Polio Syndrome a few years ago, her current athletic passion is hand cycling on a three-wheel racing bicycle. She speaks frequently on her life stories so that others can learn from her experience. Mary Lee earned her doctorate from Michigan State University while working full-time in a student services profession.

To Be Of Credit

Mary Lee Vance, Ph.D.

Unlike most Korean adoptees, I not only had to deal with racial issues, but also with disability-related issues. Somewhere between the time I was given up for adoption and adopted at age four, I contracted polio that left my legs partly paralyzed. Despite the post effects of polio, I have managed to live an active and productive life made possible through the generous support of my family and friends.

As an advisor working with other adoptees at Michigan State, I had done considerable research on adoption as it relates to loss. I learned that, in almost all cases, the birth mothers admitted to never having forgotten the child who had been given away. In almost all cases, there was incredible guilt and pain that haunted the birth mothers ruthlessly through the years. One thing that seemed to ease some of the emotional burden for the birth mothers was being reunited with their child and seeing that the child was doing fine. Even then, there was guilt and anguish over not having been able to care for their own child in the first place. This background was helpful to me years later in dealing with my own situation, when by some strange twist of fate, the brother of my birth mother tracked me down.

Despite my theoretical knowledge, one can still imagine my uncontrolled surprise, suspicion and curiosity when I was informed that my birth mother was alive and wanted to meet me. At the time of the "discovery," I was in my late 30's. Until then, I had never wasted a minute wondering about my birth family. I had resigned myself to a fate of never knowing my own biological roots based on the belief that such a search process would be hopeless in my case.

When I first became aware that biological family members were trying to reach me, I went through a wide variety of emotions. I was concerned about why they were trying to track me down now. I wondered what they needed/ wanted from me – a green card, money, or a place to live? I toyed with the idea of having everyone go through a DNA testing process, to legitimize our relationship if there was one. I was curious about what these potential new relatives would look like and concerned that maybe this would all be a big waste of time, even if they did turn out to be blood-related. Mostly I decided not to go into the situation with any expectations. This way, I would not be disappointed by the outcome.

Initially, I met my maternal uncle and his son in the U.S. When I met them, I was struck by the fact that both of them were incredibly attractive. I felt pleased to think I might be related to such good-looking people. To my relief, I learned that both had their green cards and that the son was actually in the process of getting his citizenship.

Later, when I met my birthmother and her mother in the U.S., I was again struck by their good looks. It amazed me that I might be biologically related to them. In turn, they looked at me and nodded their heads in acknowledgement. My new maternal grandmother said that I had my birth father's nose! The observation hit me like a ton of bricks. Having grown up not looking stereotypically Korean, and certainly not resembling my adoptive family, the fact that I looked like someone at all seemed suddenly miraculous.

My birth mother was reluctant to talk about my birth father. She would not tell me if he was alive or dead. She clearly did not want me knowing anything about him. As for her, she had done well. She had gone to college, and worked her way into being the CEO of a traditionally male dominated company. She had no need of any money from me.

When I met my birth mother, she cried uncontrollably. She could barely utter her first question to me which was to ask if I was upset with her. When I assured her that I wasn't angry with her, nor did I blame her for her decision to give me up, I could see a slight burden lifted. But then as she observed the results of my polio, she again began to dissolve into tears. Fresh guilt and grief swept over her. She told me that I had been perfectly healthy when I was given up. The polio had struck after she last saw me.

To feel loss for my past seems like indulging in a form of pathetic futility. What is past is past. What I do with my life in the present and the future seems more productive to me. However, while participating in the Korean War Memorial service at the First International Korean Adoptee Gathering in 1999 in Washington, D.C., I admit that I felt a sense of emotional loss for the first time in my life. Had I seen the Korean War Memorial by myself, I most likely would not have reacted as I did when surrounded by my fellow adoptees. Somehow, the sense of loss seemed magnified when with the other adoptees. Suddenly I felt remorse about not having had the opportunity to be more closely linked to my motherland.

Living in northern Virginia between 1997-2001 near Annandale (otherwise known as "Little Korea"), I had easy access to Korean grocery stores, fresh kimchi, Korean language books and other Korean goodies. I attended Smithsonian sponsored performances by Korean artists, and other Korean community coordinated activities. Additionally, I developed a frequent contact pattern with other Korean adoptees and attend several adoptee-related functions each year. In 2003

I plan to go to Korea with other Korean adoptees to help observe the 50th Anniversary of International Adoption. It will be my first trip back to Korea since I arrived in the States with my one-way ticket.

I feel strongly about the need for all people to "give back" to the community that raised them. In particular, I feel that as a Korean American adoptee, I have a responsibility to serve as a positive role model and ambassador for international adoptions as well as for the Korean American community. Regardless of how one feels politically or socially about being an adoptee, I believe it behooves Korean adoptees to keep in mind from whence we originated.

Regardless of how white we may think we act, dress or speak, to everyone else we are not white nor will we ever be considered white. We can never assimilate. At best we might be able to acculturate. As a result, we need to understand how people see us in order to help overcome the stereotypes and negative impressions people may have of us as a whole. I am keenly aware of my nationality (US citizen), race (Asian Pacific American), ethnicity (Korean American), and family status (Korean adoptee). I am also aware that I have a physical disability, and of course am female. Need I add that I am also short? In being aware of who I am and represent, I have taken the responsibility to learn what I can do to contribute to society and to give back.

So, how do I give back? Sponsoring a child

in Korea through Holt Children's Services, being active with the Korean adoptee community, speaking at adoptive parent events. I do presentations and outreach to members of the Asian Pacific American community as well as groups interested in learning more about issues related to disabilities.

Speaking openly about my adoptive as well as my birth family experiences, I attempt to be objective when my opinions are requested, and do book reviews related to a wide variety of issues connected to the Korean and/or Asian Pacific American community. I try to be a well-rounded person and a credit to my family members – both birth and adoptive, and of course, to myself.

Sunny Diaz
sunnywisdom@yahoo.com

Sunny, 26, is a public health researcher pursuing her Masters degree in Public Health and Education. She grew up speaking English and Spanish, eating tamales and menudo during the holidays in her Mexican-American family. While on a Fulbright English teaching grant in Korea, she was inspired to write "For Lee Sook Cha." In it, she pays tribute to her birth mother for "having the strength to give me up, the strength to make a decision that undoubtedly was frowned upon by others – because I know she's out there, somewhere, wondering what has become of me."

For Lee Sook Cha

Hwa Sun (Sunny) Diaz

She pushed me out of
her womb, me screaming with
a round red face and mass of wild black hair.
She held me in her arms and
toted me on her back, I imagine with
a heavy quilt wrapped around us
for warmth.

For almost a year
she held me,
touched my hair and tried to make me
say "Oh-mah",
and she fed me soft white rice
and breast milk,
gave me her blood, and showered
me with tears when she
said good-bye.

I cannot picture her smile or
remember her voice or
know what her bosom smelled like and
now I am here,

where I began, where I
took the shape and form of
"my" people.

I cannot remember if she
walked slowly or hurried, I don't know if
she stuttered when she became excited,
what kind of dreams she had as a child,
if she was afraid of the dark or being alone—
and I will never find out what
she did to make me stop crying or
what she said each morning when
she greeted me.

I do not know her.
I came from her body and
her hands used to wash me and
her lips used to touch my cheeks
and forehead.

I cannot remember ever knowing her.
And somewhere, in this country
she fights every day to keep
the memory of my face
from fading.

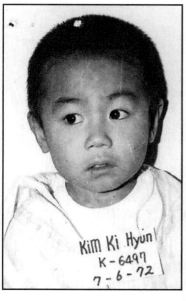

Stephen Morrison
steve@mpak.com

Steve, 46, lives in Los Angeles with his family. He had always dreamt of having a family of his own and now he is living that dream with his wife and three children, one adopted from Korea. He is an elder at the West Los Angeles Korean Church. Although an aerospace engineer by profession, his life passion and mission are with Mission to Promote Adoption in Korea (MPAK, www.mpak.com) that he founded. His message to all adoptees includes: "What matters the most is that we live for today and hope for tomorrow. Though our beginnings were not ours to choose, we can at least choose our future."

Just One of the Seeds from the East

Stephen C. Morrison

Unlike most adoptees, I remember having lived with my birth parents and a younger brother in Korea at one time. My father had a successful business and we lived in a big house. For some reason his business venture failed and he became depressed. He turned to alcohol and that was the cause of the breakup of our family. My mother left him because he often abused her physically. My father, unable to find work, soon got into a trouble with the law and was put into a prison. I was five years old and my brother, three. With both of our parents gone, we were left alone to take care of ourselves.

We lived under a bridge by a train station. Each day, we walked the streets with our heads down, not out of shame, but to find coins that people dropped. With them, we bought cookies, some rice, and other food. At night, we cuddled up under a blanket not knowing where our next meal would come from. We were too young to worry about tomorrow.

One day a vendor near the bridge took my brother home with her to raise him. I envied him and wished I could have gone with him. At least he had a place to sleep and someone would take care of him. He wouldn't be hungry any more. Unfortunately for me, that was the last time I saw my brother.

In 1962, at age 6, I was admitted to the Il-San Children's Center to have surgery on my bad knee. In those days, most of the children at Il-San Center were healthy and foreign families adopted many of them. My life there was a very happy one despite missing my brother. Harry Holt and his family lived there. Harry left the life of comfort and wealth in his Oregon farm to help homeless children in war-torn Korea.

I remember his bushy eyebrows and his big smiles. I used to run into his wide-opened arms and he would give me a firm hug. He would let me sit beside him on his earthmover as he worked the fields. Children surrounded him and called out after him wherever he went.

His wife Bertha had a blonde French braid on her hair and always walked around with a camera dangling from her neck. She took pictures with the camera that folded in and out like an accordion. Their daughter, Molly, came to Il-San after completing nursing school in America. She taught us Bible stories. She still lives and works with the children at Il-San to this day. They loved us and we loved being around them.

When Harry Holt died in 1964, he was 59 years old. I stood and watched him being buried. It rained heavily on that day. It rained also in the hearts of many who knew and loved Harry. It rained the hardest, though, in the hearts of all of us children.

I lived at Il-San for eight years and finally was adopted in 1970 at the age of fourteen. My new parents had three biological children - two girls and a boy. A year and a half before I came to the family, they adopted an Amerasian boy named James, who also came from Il-san.

Of the five Morrison children in the house, I was the most studious one. I learned the study habit while at Il-san. Early on in Korea, I realized that education could get me far in life. I aspired to be a good student. Each night after dinner, I would lock myself in a room and study. I was a nerd.

In college, I studied Aeronautical and Astronautical Engineering. Later on I received an M.S. degree in Aerospace Engineering from the University of Southern California. I am currently working on the GPS III satellite program at the Aerospace Corporation in El Segundo, California.

Growing up in the Morrison family, I always looked up to my father for his leadership and wise counsel. One day my father and I were watching TV and having a nice conversation when he looked at me very seriously. He said, "Steve, when we adopted you, we thought we were doing it because you needed parents. We adopted you because you were in need of a home. We did it to help you. However, as I look back all the years you have been with us, it is we who have been blessed more by your presence in our family."

His words moved my heart and were implanted in my memory forever. Several days later, he added, "Steve, as I look back in my life, I've made some very important decisions that turned out to be the best decisions. The best one was when I decided to believe in God. The second best decision was when I married your mother Margaret. The third best was to have you in our home." With those words, I was speechless for a while. My love and respect for my father soared that day. I shall never forget those kind words as long as I live.

Shortly after college, I was asked to serve on the Board of Directors at Holt. I was honored and privileged to serve with Grandma Holt, the founder. As a child at Il-San, not in my wildest imagination had I ever thought that one day I would join Grandma Holt in helping homeless children throughout the world. As a board member for 16 years, I learned much about adoption. During this time, I began to think about how wonderful it would be if Koreans could adopt like they do in the U.S.

I have never forgotten the faces of homeless children who remained in Korea with no families of their own. Understanding why Koreans do not adopt and finding ways to change their negative attitudes and thoughts toward adoption began to consume much of my thoughts and energy. How can I reach the Korean hearts on behalf of the homeless children? What can I say or do to change their unfavorable thoughts on adoption?

Foreign adoptions had been taking place for over 45 years but the adoption culture in Korea has hardly improved. The vast majority of the Koreans who adopted did it secretly for fear of being labeled as infertile. They were afraid of the prejudice their children might face for having been adopted. This was the cultural backdrop that I faced as I contemplated ways to promote adoption in Korea.

In 1999, I founded an organization called the Mission to Promote Adoption in Korea (MPAK). Realizing that Korea may someday stop sending children overseas, I felt a heavy burden in my heart to do something to help the children without families. I have always advocated adoption as something that is beautiful and wonderful for both children and parents.

Koreans must open their hearts and homes to homeless children. The time has come for them to abandon their centuries-old tradition and custom of taking care of only their blood relatives. MPAK was formed with these thoughts in mind and to be a voice for those homeless children remaining in Korea.

In November 1999, the Korean KBS-TV invited me to Korea to do a one-hour program on my life. KBS-TV is the largest TV station in Korea. Previously, the TV crew came to the States to tape various scenes of my family, my work, church, and my MPAK work. In Korea, they taped my visit to the Il-San Children's Center where I met with old friends who were never adopted. Some actors played the roles of my brother and I and reenacted scenes from my early childhood.

The TV program, "This is What Life is," was aired on December 2, 1999 during primetime. The program received a good rating and generated a great interest in MPAK by the viewers. I received many emails from them. According to KBS-TV, a number have called to order copies of the program and requested a second run.

KBS ran the program again a few months later. Along with the other mass media exposures, each event led me to some wonderful adoptive parents in Korea. MPAK-Korea was formed in November 1999 under the leadership of Mrs. Han, Yun Hee, who became the MPAK-Korea president.

Today MPAK has grown tremendously. What started in Southern California has spread to Korea like wild fire. Under the leadership of Mrs. Han and the cooperation of many, MPAK now has five regional branches in Seoul, Kwangju, Taegu, Taejun, and Keochang, Korea. They consist mainly of adoptive families who are not afraid to share their adoption experiences openly. Their love stories through adoptions were featured in many TV programs, magazines and newspapers.

Their positive stories in adoption gradually started to chip away the centuries-old negative social stigma regarding adoption. In addition to quarterly meetings at each branch, we have an annual national conference for adoptive parents in Korea. The last conference was a very successful one with around 600 people present. Today, it is undeniable that changes in the attitude of adoption have occurred in Korea. It still has a long way to go but we are hopeful that in 20 to 30 years, Korea will view adoption as favorably as in the U.S.

When Harry and Bertha Holt first brought over the eight "Seeds from the East," they had no idea that thousands of other seeds would follow. I am privileged to be but one of the thousands of those Seeds from the East.

Michelle Zebrowski
MeechieX@aol.com

Michelle, 19, is a junior at the University of Delaware with a major in philosophy. She was adopted at 4 and grew up in Delaware. Her first trip to Korea was in 1998 with Camp Sejong, a Korean culture camp. She is passionate about punk rock, reading, and photography. "My Omma (Mom) of Seoul" was written for her college application essay.

My Omma of Seoul

Michelle Zebrowski

Dear _____,

I don't know what to call you, and I don't know exactly where you are in this world. I do know, however, that part of you is with me. I see your reflection in my eyes. I hear your voice when I sing. I cry your tears when I cry. You are in my thoughts, yet I have no realistic pictures in my mind. I can only hope that you are safe and doing well in your unknown place.

You pervade my soul daily. I strive for excellence so that one day I may show you my accomplishments and make you proud of me. Your strength carries me as I surge to conquer my demons. I overcome humiliation by searching deep within me to find my inner pride. Most of all, I have found sacrificing my desires and facing my fears are a necessary part of love.

My sorrows and frustrations are not forgotten. These feelings haunt and betray me. They connect me to you, sometimes taking on a life of their own, disconnecting me from myself. I am often forced to take steps backwards in my journey to self-identity because of knowledge I lack.

You left me in a place with unknown consequences, so I could be taken somewhere better. Your loss in this life was for mine to have hope. We parallel each other yet we are worlds apart.

Your birth daughter, Your Seoul baby,
Michelle Zebrowski, Sung Shin Lee

Birth Father: Unknown

Kara Carlisle
(See her biography on p. 15.)

Children have fantastic imaginations. And adopted children, by nature of their own incomplete story, oftentimes create amazing characters whose lives tell wonderful tales of intrigue that any Hollywood producer would eagerly endorse. Both consciously and unconsciously are these stories woven into the identity of an adoptee and these stories live on well into adulthood. The stories are part of who we are.

While the comfort of stories to a restless child (and perhaps to a restless adult) are beacons of hope and longing that "might come true one day," coming face to face with reality, is another story altogether. In September of 2000, in a tiny welfare room somewhere in the heart of Seoul, with green furniture and cluttered shelves, the scripts authored by my "fantastic imagination" were replaced with the "true documentary" that is my life.

I was traveling with a small tour group through South Korea for 10 days when a police officer in Seoul traced a two-letter last name on my adoption papers all the way to my birth father. Ironically enough, I had never imagined meeting him. My adoption papers listed a full name for my birth mother, as well as her age, but beneath the section entitled "birth father," the words "unknown" were printed in bold, black ink.

I grew up convinced that the two letter word was a pseudo-name randomly chosen for my papers. Somewhere over time, I had even convinced myself that he did not know of my existence. After all, it was my *birth mother* who had carried me in her womb, cared enough to leave her full name, and given me life; she was the heroine of my story. So, when Dr. Kim, our tour guide, received word that my birth father had been located and was to meet me the following day, I was baffled. It was so unexpected that I collapsed into bed. I used to sleep to shield my fairy tale world from any thoughts from reality that might have had the power to penetrate my life the following day.

Dr. Kim and I arrived at the agency a bit early that Saturday morning, so we decided to freshen up before the meeting. Upon our return from the restroom, we entered the meeting room to find a Korean man, dressed in a dark charcoal suit, standing solemnly before us. Still numb, I figured it must be him, but the Korean being spoken back and forth around me left me confused about what was happening.

It was all so surreal . . . I looked at him, found out that he was my birth father, and then froze. I was not sure what to do, I could not say anything (in part because I do not speak Korean), and so I awkwardly embraced him. His body was stiff and unresponsive, his demeanor rather stoic. I could hardly believe that he was real.

We sat down, my birth father in a chair to my left, I in a chair to his right. Dr. Kim sat across from us on a matching green loveseat, with a small table in between us. The social worker sat on a stool near the doorway, watching the miraculous meeting unfold between two strangers.

I cannot be sure of what all happened there. Time and events seem so scattered as I think back to those first few moments. I remember Dr. Kim snapping pictures. I remember how my once calm, controlled, "scripted" demeanor began to transform, from composed silence and dry eyes to tiny, salty tear drops, and then to a quaking body pouring forth a raging river of emotion.

As I sat there in that tiny room, I let go of my usually suppressed feelings for the first time in my life. I was not ashamed to recognize and express the deep longings to know from whom I had come. And, finally, I was not willing to shrug off my need to know if those who had first given me life had wanted me.

As the Korean conversations slowed, Dr. Kim

invited me into the conversation and the social worker, Ms. Park, began to speak to me. The first thing she said was, "He says you look just like your mother . . . even your hands." (So that is why he grabbed my hands as I sat down in the chair next to him.) She continued on to tell me that I reminded him of her—my outgoing and friendly spirit and my intelligence. It was amazing to look at his face and see mine; it was surreal to imagine my spirit as part of hers.

As the conversation ensued, I finally decided to ask the obvious question: "Can you please tell me the story of my birth?" He took a deep breath as I emotionally began to brace myself to hear the true story about my life. He paused and then began remembering back to when he first met my birth mother. . .

He was in his mid-twenties and a traveling photographer who spent much of his time taking senior pictures. He and my birth mother met during her senior year attending a business high school in Seoul. Drawn to her outgoing and friendly demeanor, he asked her out. This led to a three year dating relationship.

During the years, she became pregnant. At the time of my delivery, my birth parents were struggling with how to take care of me since I had been conceived out of wedlock. In Korean society, as was the case in the United States fifty years ago, an illegitimate birth was not only considered unacceptable but very shameful to a family. One of the nurses at the hospital heard them talking and eventually helped connect my birth mother to the welfare agency.

As it turns out, I was born prematurely and then kept in the hospital. My birth father left me there unresolved about the situation and returned to the hospital three days later to check on me—only to find that I had "been taken care of." He had signed nothing and did not know what it meant, that I had "been taken care of." He was uncertain as to whether I was alive or dead. As it turns out, my birth mother, while she signed me over to the welfare agency, was also uncertain about my future.

After the pregnancy, my birth parents stayed together for a while as my birth father continued to travel about looking for photography work. During that period he said that they "naturally grew apart." There were no fights or great conflicts—mere life circumstances caused them to drift apart.

Not long after their breakup his parents began to pressure him to marry. While he was reluctant to pursue marriage, it was expected of him as the first son. So, his mother introduced him to a woman whom he married. One month after his wedding my birth mother reappeared but it was too late for them.

Later on, she married another man. She contacted my birth father eight years ago. At that time, they visited and talked about my birth. As was the case with my birth father, my birth mother had also kept my birth a secret. He finished his story by saying that they had had no contact since then and he had no way to contact her at that time.

After the meeting with my birth father, I left Seoul with an email address uncertain as to the future of our relationship. He eventually told his wife and family and, through a series of inside connections, we were able to secretly contact my birth mother. While I have been flown back to Seoul to meet my birth father's extended family very openly, a twenty-five minute, secret meeting with my birth mother is the totality of my contact with her. Those few minutes will likely be the only ones I will ever have with her. Meetings are dangerous, her past unacceptable in her present life and our lives inevitably separated by custom and continent.

I still struggle with letting go of the dream of her as my heroine and my childhood renditions of our separation. I still am trying to absorb the fact that I will never see her again. And, while the warm embrace of my birth father and his entire family is much more like any fairy tale that I could have created, the complexity of new relationships is at times overwhelming. Wrestling with the dissonant realities of pain and guilt, relationships and rejection, and questions and answers, are less comforting in many ways than living out of my imaginary world. Living in the ambiguity, with expectancy and intrigue, seems easier and freer at times.

I continue to work at opening up my white-knuckled fists and letting go of the stories that I had grasped to sustain me. I am now realizing that the truth of my life will only become manifest as I learn how to trust, not the constructs of a sophisticated imagination, but real life.

True freedom will be achieved when I am able to let go of the script, hold hands with real people, and trust again.

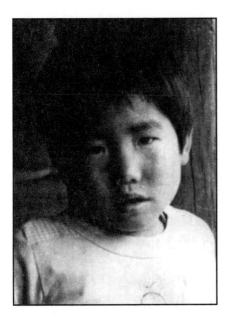

Jung-Hoe Hopgood
jhopgood@hotmail.com

Jung-Hoe, 24, is an engineer passionate about environmental ethics and philosophy. His interests vary from singing and sports to writing and computer. His parents of German descent adopted him at age 5. "What's in a Name?" was written soon after his last of three trips to Korea. Since then, he continues to study Korean culture and language. Jung-Hoe is an active member of Korean Presbyterian Church in Southfield, Michigan.

What's in a Name?

Jung-Hoe Hopgood

My life has consisted of several stages. Each stage has actually correlated to a likewise literal transformation in identity or rather, development toward a Korean-American identity. Over the years I have been known by different names.

When I first arrived in my new adoptive family at the age of 5, my parents tried calling me by my Korean name on the child referral. Their first attempts to call me were ignored when they called my name by "Jung-Ho," and I repeatedly indicated to them that my name was something sounding like "Jung-Ha." This was my first identity established in America and became my concept of self for the first 15 years.

In grade school, I was very rambunctious. I never really noticed a difference among my classmates although I was one of the few Asians in school. It was probably stressed to me to conform and almost prove how "American" I was even though I had a Korean name.

My college years formed the second stage when I had a great exposure to a relatively few Koreans but was able to make lasting, close friendships with them. At this stage, I learned my name in Korean was really "Jung-Ho." Most of my college friends know me as Jung-Ho and my hometown friends as Jung-Ha.

My third stage wasn't realized until I made a return trip to Korea where I found my worn documents at the baby reception home in Kwangju, Korea. It was written that my name was really "Jung-Hoe" (pronounced "Jung Hway"). This is supposed to be my true name but it couldn't be verified as my given name because it was common for orphanage directors to name children who had been abandoned. However, it was very amazing to see so many Koreans attempting to empathize and willing to come to my aid in my search for identity.

In my professional life as an environmental engineer, my Korean background has had little visible influence. I am not certain about the number of people who may have been deterred, intimidated or changed their attitude upon seeing me but I have never directly felt I was discriminated against. My first name is foreign sounding and this alone may impact other's perception of me on paper prior to ever seeing me.

In the summer of my freshman year of college, I was first hired by the company I work for now. I joined under the name of "John" because it seemed pretty difficult for new people to pronounce my name correctly upon introduction, and I had assumed it would only be temporary summertime employment. As a consequence, John was added to all my other aliases. Even today, the survey department still knows me as John and the rest of my co-workers know me as Jung-Hoe.

My transition with names reflects my gradual realization of who I am and my unique situation. Currently, I feel a great pride in being Korean, which I wasn't able to say 5 years ago or even a year before. I also feel more fulfilled and believe that I have a purpose with real meaning.

As a result of my trip to Korea in 1998, I am more fully aware of common links to both societies. I am fortunate to have left Korea for a better life in America. I am fortunate to be Korean and share the blood of my ancestors who persevered under such hardship as the May 18 Kwangju Massacre. I was found wandering the streets of Kwangju following a civil unrest that ultimately resulted in a very bloody massacre of many leaders, protesters and innocent citizens.

Here is a poem I wrote in my journal upon my first return trip to my homeland, traveling a brief 12 hours around the earth, and emerging in a former culture and life that was once my own.

Overcoming Distance, Merging Space, Reconciling Time

Crossing a span
Half a day away.
My new life freezes
As my former resumes.

Fast forwarding 15 years
With 20 years of wisdom.
I visit my former self
Barely able to understand.

Continuing in my old duties
Playing with friends.
Laughing again
But my memory fails.

This place is so foreign
My belongings dispersed.
This person I once was
No longer remains.

Initial impressions are made
Traveling the old path once more.
A little less steady
A slight bit unsure.

On this world of mine
Both sides I emerged.
Yet I have somehow found
My own way home.

Now I know that
I will always be welcomed.
On this small Earth
On both sides of day.

I have come full circle
To where I began my journey.
So distant, yet so close
In just a 12 hour flight.

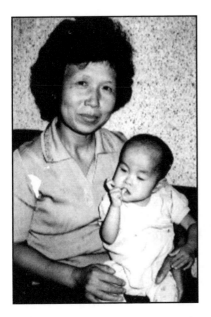

Asia Renning
Arenning@aol.com

Asia, 21, is a runner who has run every day for over 1100 days. Many awards have been won for her school track and cross country teams and in the Special Olympics. She did not start walking, though, until age 2 when she was adopted. Asia was born with Hirschprung's Disease and is autistic. Currently, she is a student in Young Adults Pilot Program at Washtenaw Community College in Michigan. Her mother writes her story.

Against All Odds

Asia and Adair Renning

Although a late starter in the walking department, shortly after mastering the skill, Asia had learned to run and, since that time, preferred running and jumping to walking. In backyard races, she beat her older sister soundly and always left the other kids in the dust on the playground. By the time Asia was in middle school, my husband, Jerry, and I knew we wanted to channel that energy but the athletic program did not allow runners to start until the seventh grade. We waited.

In the spring of 1996, Asia joined the track team and began going to workouts after school. She loved the running and being with other girls. In early March of that year, after dropping our two daughters off at school, I heard an announcement on the radio about nominating people to carry the Olympic Torch. To nominate someone, you had to write, in twenty-five worlds or less, why that person deserved to carry the

Torch as it passed through Detroit on its way to the Atlanta Games.

The deadline to enter was that day — March 8th. I raced home to the computer to enter online. Jerry and I wrote: "Asia has used music and cross country running to help battle autism. Her colostomy doesn't slow her down." The following Monday a representative from the radio station called to say that, out of hundreds of entries, Asia had been selected to carry the Torch for 5/8 of a mile.

The next few months went by in a blur of excitement and preparation. Asia competed on the track team and ran in Special Olympics. On the weekends, Jerry taught her to run with a baseball bat to get her used to running with something in her hand. Later, we bought lawn torches so she would be used to running with something flaming. Almost daily, the mail brought forms to sign, information to review, and videos on the preparations.

Each runner was allowed an escort, a job her Dad gladly accepted. Finally their uniforms arrived and we were given the location of the 5/8-mile segment. We drew up maps and sent them to our friends. Jerry's parents arrived the day before and we all went to watch as the Torch passed through Monroe, MI, near our home town of Milan, the night before Asia's run.

The day dawned gray and drizzling but warm as we left for downtown Detroit at 5:30 a.m. to meet with the Olympic team that would work with us and the other runners throughout the event. In all, there were eighty-five runners in our area, each nominated by different organizations for different reasons. We had already met the person who would pass the flame to Asia and the one to whom she would pass the flame.

Our family and friends, twenty-two strong, waited on the corner of Willis and Woodward for the previous runner to pass the flame from his Torch to Asia. Then she was gone, running down Woodward, the main street in Detroit, with Jerry on one side, the official escort runner on the other, and four uniformed motorcycle escorts forming a box around them all. The crowd erupted in cheers.

The cameras that were on a truck immediately in front of her filmed Asia's entire run. So we all got to see what everyone else had seen — Asia running at a comfortable pace, proudly holding the Torch, with her father beside her. Then we saw she passed the flame on to the next runner.

On the day after the Relay, Asia sat down to write a thank-you to everyone involved, from the radio station that chose her to run to Coca-Cola Bottling Company who sponsored the Relay and to the people who cheered for her. Here is her letter:

Asia's Thank You Letter

Thank You WHYT People for Picking me To Carry The Torch.

Thank You Coca-Cola Bill Holl for The Nice Party at The Fox Theater and the Bag of Goodies.

It Was Fun to Meet Chuck Gaidica and Mayor Archer and shake Hands.

Thank You For Seeing Carmen Harlan and Rideing on bus Number 8.

Thank You People For Coming To See Olympic Torch.

Thank You Dertians For Coming and Watch me Run The Torch.

Thank You Dad To Run With Me. Thank You.

Thank You Mom for Sending My Name in To Carry The Olympic Torch.

Thank You Jess Spike For Coming and Taking The Pictures.

Thank You For Takeing Movies Meghann and For Being My Sister.

Thank You Cleon and Lorena For Coming To Watch me Run The Torch.

Thank You Paul and Judy and Ben and Rachel Spike For Coming and watch me Run The Torch. And Holding my Middle School Sign.

Thank You Larry Walker For putting fire to My Olympic Torch.

Thank You Grandma and Papa Renning To Come and Cheer For Me.

Thank You Mrs. Truslow and Coach Porter and Mrs. Underwood.

Thank You Ursula for Taking The Flame.

Thank You Kathy and Wayne For Coming and Taking Nice Pictures and to put them in My computer.

Thank You People Who Rode The Torch Bus.

Lots of People Was Glad to Watch Me Run The Torch.

That's What I'm Telling Mayor David Ludwig. You Gave me a Nice Award.

The Milan Middle-School Kids did Not Come to Watch Me Run The Olympic Torch But They made Me a Big Beautiful Sign For Me.

Thank You God For Making Me Healthy To Run.

Love Asia Renning

The thoughts, typing, and spelling are all Asia's. A little help with punctuation is provided by Adair Renning, her mother.

120

Paull Shin, Ph.D.
shin pa@leg.wa.gov

Paull (Shin, Ho Bom), 66, is the first Korean-American to be elected a state senator. Adopted over 40 years ago, he transformed himself from a street urchin in Korea to an American political leader. He was guided by one thing – a passion for learning. Having had no formal education in Korea, he started working on his GED at age 18 and eventually earned his Ph.D. His dream in life was to become a "useful person," who can make contributions to others and to society.

American Blessings

Paull Shin, Ph.D.

I, for one, consider it a great blessing to have been adopted. I was born in Korea, and at the age of four, my mother died. Shortly thereafter, my father left me. Having no place to go, I became a street urchin, standing on the street corners of Seoul begging for food to stay alive until age 15. When the Korean War broke out in 1950, I fled to the south to avoid the communists. Rumor had it that the US forces were landing in Inchon so I decided to walk up to the front and greet the arriving American troops.

As the soldiers came from south of the Han River trying to cross north, US army engineers built emergency rubber rafts for a bridge. As the convoys of hundreds of vehicles passed across the bridge, I was one of hundreds of homeless kids waving at the soldiers. "Hallo, chewing gum. Hallo, chocolate" hoping they would throw candy to us. One day, for reasons unknown, one of the soldiers lent me his hand and, as I reached out to him, he picked me up and brought me over to the truck. It was this simple gesture that constituted the beginning of my new life.

The US Army took an interest in me. Upon crossing over into Seoul, they placed me with a unit of seven Army officers as a houseboy. I began my first and new career polishing shoes and washing and ironing their clothes. One of the officers, Dr. Ray Paull, an Army dentist, took a special interest in me. He and his family eventually adopted me and brought me to the United States at age 18.

After my first dinner in America, my Dad asked me what I would like to do. My immediate response was, "Father, I would like to be educated." Unfortunately for me, the prospect of school was not that easy. I had never gone to school in Korea. The next day, we visited a grade school and a junior high only to be rejected for being too old. As a last resort, we went to a local high school.

The principal looked at me and said, "You have no grade school education, no junior high school education, how can I possibly take you?" I was so disappointed and emotionally hurt that I burst into tears. The principal asked why I was crying. I replied, "Sir, one of the reasons I came here was to get an education, but getting an education has become an impossible dream for me." He then told me about the special program called the GED for boys like me.

With the help of a wonderful special tutor and the support of my parents, I not only passed the GED but also went on to a university, continued on to graduate school for a Master's Degree, and a Ph.D. from the University of Washington.

I consider myself living proof of American blessings and opportunity. In the course of my education, I came upon a passage from Benjamin Franklin, who said, "A grateful person is one who realizes blessings and reciprocates by serving." Having received so many blessings in this country, I decided to serve. I embarked on a teaching career that has spanned over 31 years

Teaching students is extremely gratifying when you see that your words and actions are a benefit to others and will help them prepare for life. I was called on by governors of Washington State to serve as an advisor on trade issues and led several trade missions to various Asian countries. I was grateful that I was able to render service to the people of the United States and Asia.

I have been active in a number of community organizations such as the United Way, the Boy Scouts of America and the YMCA. I have also been keenly involved in international adoption organizations such as World Association of Children and Parents (WACAP), Holt, and Korean Identity Development Society (KIDS), which I co-founded to assist adoptees in adjusting to life in the United States.

I cannot say that my experience is exceptional. Indeed, there are many Korean adoptees in the United States who have found successful, meaningful lives and many ways to contribute to the betterment of their communities. However, as a minority living and working in the United States, my experience was not without many problems and obstacles.

One of the challenges often confronting me was the simple question, "Who am I?" People would ask me if I am Japanese. I'd say "no". They'd ask me if I was Chinese. I'd say "no". Then they'd ask, "Well, what are you then?" To that question I'd answer, "I'm an American." Their reply was always, "Oh, no, no, I mean who are your ancestors?"

This was a very uncomfortable question for me because, no matter how I tried to become American, somehow I was always labeled a minority. This is one of the main problems adoptees face, not only adoptees but also most international minority groups in the United States. The struggles and experiences they have in order to find their own identity are shared by many of us. "Where do I belong?" "What should I do?" "What is my identity?" are questions with which many minority groups struggle.

When I left Korea, I vowed never to return again because of the discrimination and suffering that I endured. I came to the United States with a new attitude and a new purpose — to seek the rainbow I had heard was the American

Dream. I tried my hardest to become part of my adopted family who had shown me so much love and attention, but the society around me was not nearly as hospitable as my family. Society continued to question my ability to become an American.

As I searched for my own identity, I discovered that in order to find my true self, I had to seek out my heritage. Through studying the language, history and culture of Korea, I was able to understand my unique background and relate that to my present situation. In doing so, I was able to reconcile with myself and understand my role in this hybrid society that was the United States.

Although one can be adopted and loved by a caring family, it is impossible to change one's color; I will always be a Korean-American. However, I learned to assimilate myself in the American mainstream and found positive ways to contribute to this society. Being a teacher helped me understand that many issues are associated with identity and discrimination.

Having found my identity, I decided the best way to pay back to this country was through public service. I felt that serving in politics was one of the fastest ways to be integrated into the mainstream. I had never run for a public office, but in 1992, I decided to run for a seat in the Washington State Legislature.

My opponent was a four-term incumbent and a well-known man in the district. In addition, the district in which I lived was comprised of over 95% white Americans. My friends, associates and the press all told me it was an impossible dream. Nevertheless, I had a strong will and desire to serve.

I visited every home in the district that summer, telling constituents my story of success and American opportunity. I testified to them that it was time for me to pay back society for the blessings I have received. When November finally came, I won the election by an 11% margin, to the astonishment and surprise of many.

Although I was surprised by the result, I had a startling revelation in the course of the campaign. I realized that I was afraid to run for public office because of my color. Deep down in my heart, I did not believe that I could be fully accepted by the American people. Fortunately, my victory proved that the fear I had was only fear itself.

In 1998, I won a seat in the Washington State Senate again using the same campaign approach. I went through 4 pairs of shoes walking every day, 9 hours a day, for 9 months, soliciting the vote of neighbors and other people I so desperately wanted to serve. This only proves that one can overcome anything with the right spirit and determination.

Everyone must have a dream of some kind — a dream and a belief that you are God's child, and a belief in yourself and your capacity to become anything and everything you desire. The power of positive thinking and the conviction that you can achieve your dream cannot be underestimated. I learned this valuable lesson as I went from feeling like a nobody to feeling a strong sense of accomplishment and acceptance.

One must understand that adoption is a blessing. You've probably heard the saying that "blood is thicker than water." This is true but my testimony to you is that "love is thicker than blood." It is that love you possess through your adoptive family, you become one of them, and you share love by giving and receiving. It is the love that conquers all. If you first have love for yourself, you can begin to love others and feel a desire to serve your fellow men.

My advice to adoptees and Asians in the United States is simply to work at loving yourself and believe that you are equal in capacity and potential to anyone else. With this attitude, and with a lot of hard work and prayerful determination, any dream can become a reality.

Lee Lind
lee_naeyean@hotmail.com

Lee, 34, aka Lee Nae-Yean, has returned to her Motherland Korea to begin a new chapter in her life. She works in the Post Adoption Services section of Holt Children's Services in Seoul. Her responsibilities are to assist the return adult adoptees with their background search and to help the birth parents who want to reunite with their children. This work has been very rewarding to her in defining her identity. Lee lives with her biological sister and a niece. She feels that all of her challenges in life including her struggles during adolescence have made her to be a stronger adult.

Who am I?

Lee Lind

As I journeyed through life, I was presented with many different types of questions. I just could not believe that the majority of the questions were from myself to me, Lee.

Whenever I was registering to vote, and even while I was signing up for university classes, I encountered confusing moments. I would be required to fill out an application form, and these forms have spaces for:

FIRST NAME, LAST NAME, ADDRESS, TELEPHONE NUMBER, WORK PHONE NUMBER, AND DATE OF BIRTH, etc.

I get through the first part smoothly. Then comes the section where I have to make a decision; it has a space for:

OPTIONAL: CHECK THE BOX WHICH BEST DESCRIBES YOURSELF: AFRICIAN-AMERI-

CAN; ASIAN/PACIFIC ISLANDER; CAUCASIAN; LATINO; NATIVE AMERICAN; OTHER.

Once I reach this part, I am like a writer with a major writer's block. I begin brainstorming. How do I best describe myself within the confines of the choices listed? Should I check the space next to the Asian/Pacific Islander since it does contain the word "Asian?"

My personal history is that I was born in South Korea and had 12 years of life in Korea. On the other hand, since I was adopted to the United States, I have an American family and an American citizenship. Yet, I cannot mark the box labeled "Caucasian" since I do not look Caucasian.

Just exactly who is the person that should be described on that form? I have seen changes in myself where I have lost bits of "Korean-ness" and have become Americanized.

Maybe my choice should be the box labeled "other" and I can explain the fact that I am a Korean adoptee. Do others have this dilemma? Hmm... Is it only me? All I wanted to do was vote or attend a university.

Without thinking much longer, I usually go with my first instinct, Asian/Pacific Islander. I am not sure if this is the right space but all I care about at that moment is to be finished with that difficult section. Ahaaaa, what a relief! I then silently hope that I would not have to face that type of situation again in the future but is that realistic?

With experiences like this, I am compelled to ask myself, "Who really am I?" If I could step outside of myself and have to describe Lee, how would I describe Lee? What are my true feelings about myself? How do others view me?

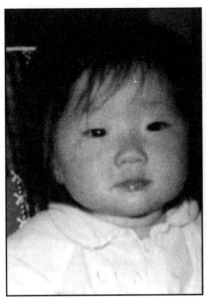 

Shannon O'Neill
soneill86@hotmail.com

Shannon, 25, loves to travel and meet people from different countries and cultures. She enjoys reading, writing, playing golf and tennis, and learning new things. A training specialist at a medical company, Shannon also is active in the Mentor & Mentee program for internationally adopted youth through Children's Home Society of Minnesota. With a B.A. in psychology and an M.A. in human resource development, she is currently pursuing her M.B.A. "Finding My Seoul" was written after her first visit to Seoul, Korea.

Finding My Seoul

Shannon E. O'Neill

At age 24, I have finally embraced being Korean. I was adopted when I was six months old and throughout my life, I never really gave much thought to being Korean. During high school and college, I made a point of avoiding Asian or multicultural groups or associating with anything or anyone that made me "stand out" or point out the fact that I was Korean. I was very uncomfortable being around other people that looked like me or emphasize the fact that I looked "different."

These feelings, or this "avoidance," continued throughout college. After college, I started talking with one of my few Korean adopted friends. We started discussing Korea and how we'd both like to see Korea. Prior to that day, I had never really given much thought to going to Korea to find out more about my heritage.

That summer, I met and talked with more

Korean adoptees. It was amazing how much we had in common! For the first time, I didn't have to tell the long-winded story about how I was born in Korea but adopted and raised in the U.S. We discussed feelings, views, issues and challenges we had faced. At first, I was nervous meeting and spending time with so many other Asians. Kind of ironic since I am Asian!

I enjoyed hearing about other adoptees' experiences in Korea. I found a friend who was also interested in seeing Korea so, within four months of starting to think about my culture and background, I had booked a flight to Korea.

I had so many emotions racing through my mind. Was I crazy to just dive into this? How would I be accepted in this country I was born in and left 23 years ago? How would I feel surrounded by Koreans? Was I going to search for my birth mother? So many questions and very few answers.

As the time grew closer, I started to question why I was going. Was I really ready for this? Would I feel a connection to the country, culture and people? I tried to prepare myself by talking to people who had been to Korea, reading travel guides and books on adoption, and looking on the Internet. Although I felt more prepared, I didn't feel completely confident that it was the right time for me to go.

My friends and family were all very supportive as I went through the roller coaster of emotions. My biggest question was how I would react when I got off the plane in Seoul and saw all these faces that looked like mine. I was so used to being "different" that I didn't know how it would feel being the "same."

After landing in Seoul, Korea, I was hit with a variety of feelings. I was excited, anxious, nervous, and uneasy. I can't begin to describe how it felt to see everyone with dark hair and eyes that looked like mine. At first, everything was overwhelming, the crowds, the people, the fast paced city. Many people would talk to me in Korean and I tried to explain that I only spoke English.

My worst fear was that people would be disappointed when they discovered I was raised in the United States, but overall, everyone that I met was very understanding and helpful. Some people wondered why I didn't know the language, culture or like the food. Some thought I had moved to the United States with my Korean parents and was raised speaking English. I felt uncomfortable having to explain that I was adopted. Again, I had fears that I would not be accepted or be a disappointment.

I had made an appointment to visit the orphanage I was at and review my file. At first, this was not something I wanted to do. I had come to the United States when I was six months old and was told that there was no information on my birth parents. I figured I was better off not knowing anything. I had never really thought about doing a search since I didn't have any information to start searching with.

I also knew that if I went all the way to Korea and didn't stop at the orphanage and see my file that I would regret it later on. Again, this is a situation I could not emotionally prepare for. I was scared to go and see my file and really confirm that they had no information on me. I met with a social worker who was very nice and helpful. We looked through my file and discussed the possibility of trying to search for my foster mother. Unfortunately, they were unable to find her since she had moved outside of Seoul.

I also met the founder of the orphanage. This was something that has dramatically impacted on my life. He was the kindest man I have ever met and I often think about him when I think of Korea. He was so happy to see that I had had a good childhood and was happy and healthy. I also had the opportunity to see some of the babies there and help out in the nursery. Words can't begin to describe all of the emotions I felt that day.

In the past year of my life, I feel like I have really grown. I can finally embrace my culture and my past and feel comfortable saying that I am Korean. I have looked into searching for my birth parents and now have closure that I know everything there is to know. I know that I would not be here today, doing the things I am doing, without the support of my family and friends.

I have been raised American and now I know that I am also Korean.

Robert Ogburn
staticvoid@hotmail.com

Robert, 42, is a Foreign Service Officer serving as a press and cultural attaché to the U.S. Consulate General in Ho Chi Minh City, Vietnam. In his career, he has been involved with the NATO Summit, Middle East Peace Talks, and has worked at the U.S. Embassy in Seoul. Born as Woo, Chang-jae in a small village north of Seoul, he grew up on the east coast of the U.S. His first novel, _Baltimore Gnostics_, was translated as _Monggae_ in Korean and sold over 40,000 copies. Robert and his wife, Thu-hang, have two children.

Quantum Leaping

Robert Ogburn

Remember Sam, the engineer-turned-time traveler on that old show, "Quantum Leap"? One week he would find himself in the body of an elderly African-American man fighting prejudice in the Old South and another week he would be a Vietnam veteran returning home after a long absence. Sam would change the course of that person's history, averting tragedy or reuniting lost love, and then he would disappear into the vortex of time and reappear in the body of yet another person in crisis.

Do you, as an adoptee, sometimes do the double take that Sam does when he looks in the mirror and sees a face peering back at him which may strike you as looking very different from the soul within?

Oh, come on, admit it.

You are getting ready to go to school or work

and you're humming a catchy tune or maybe turning over in your mind the latest George W. Bushism and then you peer into the mirror and think, "Is that face mine?" And when you do think that, some days you just sense a hint of irony and maybe other days you'd prefer just glancing at your watch and getting going.

This odd double-take doppelganger does not happen to me very often but it did hit me this morning. I was walking into my school, a couple of minutes late as usual, and I ducked into the restroom to wash my hands. I was trying to remember two or three of the Vietnamese phrases I had learned the day before, here at the Foreign Service Institute of the US State Department. However my mud-thick English accent did nothing to beautify my grasp of the lilting tones that I am sure I will hear in my next diplomatic post in Ho Chi Minh City. I looked into the mirror and a mirthful Korean face peered back at me. "Who is that guy?" I mused to myself.

There have been times, like back in high school, when I much preferred just to look away from the mirror and go back out with my white and black friends. It was much easier, as a teenager in rural Maryland, to go along with all my friends who believed, "We're all Americans and we're all the same, so who wants to fool around with the past or with foreign places?"

I put on my Quantum Leap identity because I was sure I had no other worth exploring. I knew where I was from (the Chesapeake Bay area, not the vicinity of the Han-kang), who I was (Robert Ogburn, not Woo Chang-jae), and where I was going (somewhere on my own efforts, not as part of a group package). I was happy and comfortable with this handle on my life and I did not tamper with it until college.

When I started attending the University of Maryland Baltimore County, for the first time I walked through dorm halls and sat in class with people who looked a lot like me but they definitely did not think or act like me. Since all of the Koreans on campus were very new to America, they viewed me as an amnesiac, one who looks Korean but has the misplaced brain and experiences of a stranger.

In an effort to remedy my condition, one new friend invited me to his room and pulled out of his fridge an aromatic bowl of kimchi and fish; another friend enlisted me in his crusade to skewer the campus paper for alleging that Koreans still ate canine-flavored stew; a mild classroom chat with a Korean co-ed brought out a remark by her that we could not ever get married because our family names were similar.

Amidst the new sensations and perplexities there were some golden moments, though: trying bulgogi for the first time and realizing it was the best food I had ever tasted; exploring the history of Korea as a tough, spirited shrimp among whales; gaining a modicum of tact and graciousness in talking to girls from Asian backgrounds. At college I was able to look into the mirror and begin to recognize the face staring backing at me.

Seven years later—after college, grad school, stints in investment banking, law enforcement and broadcasting—I had entered the US Foreign Service and was walking down the steps from a United Airlines flight that had just landed at Kimpo International Airport in Seoul. It was August and the air was as stifling as the humidity of Foggy Bottom, but it hit me that these were the first draughts of Seoul air to fill my lungs since I was a baby in the arms of my American mom and dad.

Fragments of another life flashed through my mind: my mom, Beccy Ogburn, hanging a small Korean flag in my childhood bedroom ("You're American, but always be proud that you started out in Korea"); those first whiffs of kimchi back in college; a Korean movie with English subtitles that I had seen about a monk who dreams an entire life in one night.

Before I left the States, my mom took me to the bank and handed me some papers from our safe deposit box. One of them, yellowed and brittle from age, was a document listing my original Korean name, Woo, and my birth mom's name. It listed my birthplace as a village north of Seoul and it had the name of the adoption agency.

With this information, I tried during my five years to play amateur detective looking for clues

143

to who my birth mom was and whether she was still alive. Mrs. Lee Yun-sook, a wonderful lady who worked at the Embassy at the time, took me to the social services agency that had handled my adoption. The name of the agency had changed, and the Director was sad to tell me that most of their older records had been destroyed.

Mrs. Lee was still determined. We enlisted the help of a mutual friend, Mr. Park, who said, "Let's go to the village listed on your adoption documents." On a Saturday morning I went with Mr. Park and my wife to the village of Chang-pa in Musan country, about 10-15 miles northwest of Seoul. We veered from paved roads onto a long dirt road leading through the center of the village. Small cement buildings with mom-and-pop stores and small businesses lined both sides of the road. We asked around and found the house in the village that was the social center for the elderly.

"Does anybody remember if a baby named Woo Chang-jae ever lived here?" Mr. Park asked. One of the oldest gentlemen there said that he remembered a Woo family but they moved some years ago and no one had kept in touch with them. From there, we tried other ways, such as checking for anyone in Korea with my mom's name, and finally doing TV and newspaper interviews. There were several leads but none panned out.

The wonderful thing is that, even though I did not find my birth parents, I felt as if the whole country adopted me as a lost son returned home.

144

Dong-a Ilbo, for example, used the proverb, "returning home in golden robes," to describe an orphan who returned as a diplomat. Since my life in America had been far removed from suffering or hardship, it was tough for me to grasp this sentiment, but it was very assuring to feel welcomed "back."

I was disappointed not to find more clues about my past, but I am glad that I went on the journey. I would like to provide some modest advice for you if you are planning a trip to Korea to search for your roots:

- Go with low expectations. I do not know what the statistics are but it is possible that you will not be able to locate a family member. Or if you do find a relative, he or she may not be living in the world's most pleasant circumstances. There is also the possibility that the family member may be in a situation in which it is very awkward to acknowledge publicly his or her relationship to you. If you are mentally prepared for any of these possibilities, you have a much better chance for a successful visit.

- Remember that success is internal. While it would certainly be wonderful if you were to make contact with Korean family members, what should be important is how you will grow and mature from the experience. If you are like me, you will feel a fuller person and the face that looks back at you in the mirror

145

will seem far less incongruous. You will probably also be much better at understanding where your individual identity fits into the rest of American society and to appreciate your uniqueness.

- Stay anchored. It is very difficult to have a "sudden" mom, dad or sibling pop into your life, so it helps tremendously to be able to share your feelings or thoughts with a close friend or relative back in the States. Having someone to talk with can be especially helpful if you are faced with a major decision— what if you do meet your biological mom, and she wants to visit you in the States or maybe even move back with you?

These are just thoughts from a fellow pilgrim, someone probably like you—and like the Quantum Leaping Sam—who knows that there are some things that are very difficult to leave behind.

Jo Rankin

Jo (Jung Im Hong), 35, born in Inchon, grew up in San Diego and earned a degree in journalism. She co-edited _Seeds from the Silent Tree: An Anthology by Korean Adoptees_ where her poem, "Biological Mother," first appeared. Her hobbies include poetry, piano, violin and chess. The two current poems depict her feelings about her two Moms — biological and adoptive.

Biological Mother

Jo Rankin

You tried your best
To cut the cord.
Destroyed a nest
Beyond afford.
My fate was filed
And soon defined:
A lonely child
You left behind.
Since you and I
May never be
Together in
Reality,
Should I go on
And try to solve
The questions which
Have since evolved,
Or should I quit
While I'm ahead
And try to do
Without, instead?
Such simple words
For mother's pearl.
From me, with love,
Your Inchon girl.

Mom

Jo Rankin

You tried your best
To fill our void,
Then built a nest
We both enjoyed.
My fate improved —
Was redefined
When Inchon soil,
I left behind.
Since you and I
Will always be
Together for
Eternity,
I finally tried
To reach resolve
With questions which
Have since dissolved.
Now I can move
And look ahead
And share my life
With you, instead.
Such simple words
For mommy's heart.
From me, with love,
Your counterpart.

Laura Cromey
ljcromey@mac.com

Laura was adopted from Korea at age four along with her twin sister. At the venerable age of 29, she is currently working as a systems analyst at a large financial company and hopes to be a very popular science fiction writer some day. Her passions include writing, reading history books, watching chopsaki and anime. Really bad science fiction films with a little skydiving and kickboxing are thrown in for active fun.

They Just Paint

LJ Cromey

When we are young we are taught that blue is the color of the sky. Green is the color of leaves and yellow is the color of the sun. And we trust in these things because it is what our parents and teachers have told us and we trust them. And so we name the trees green, the sea blue and the sun yellow.

Later they teach us about the things we have labeled. We learn that the sea is cold, the sun is hot and that trees provide shade. And we trust in those things they have told us because we trust them. But eventually we learn on our own and from others that trees can be gold, blue lies at the center of some of the hottest flames and yellow is also the color of lemonade.

And then we learn more contradicting things. We learn that there are more colors than we can name in shades and hue. We learn that others do not necessarily see colors as we see them, good, bad or indifferent. We learn on our own that sights of others can betray and nothing can judge beauty for us better than our own eyes.

Between the time we are children and the time we reach adulthood, there is confusion every time something doesn't fit inside what we've previously learned. But once we are adults and have explored our world and have reached beyond the boundaries of the categories as children, we are free to appreciate the nuances and contradictions. And we understand why we were given the original categories.

When I was little I was confident in my identity. I knew who I was. I was like my parents, of course. They were white of an Anglo Saxon ethnicity. It shouldn't have mattered that I looked different. Inside I was the same. So I busily colored myself white, and called other people who would try to tell me different, racist.

Then I grew older and found out why people of my ethnicity were wonderful. I learned of a proud history and ancient culture. I saw injustice and struggle and realized the difference between my parents' experience growing up in this world and mine. Looks did matter because my ethnicity was a part of who I was inside.

So I busily colored myself yellow and told people who would try to tell me different, prejudiced. I became angry. I felt betrayed. I felt lied to. In every stage of my becoming who I am, each time I learned a new lesson, I became more confused. Then I reached adulthood and realized that all the lessons were true.

My ethnicity is Korean. The culture I was raised in was Anglo-Saxon. I claim rightful heritage to both. I have learned the prides and pitfalls of two worlds that are both ugly and beautiful. I was rejected and embraced by both and I embraced and rejected them in kind. In doing so, I found that, though they are each an essential part of me, they do not define who I am.

Ethnicity is both meaningful and meaningless. It is still one I wrestle with everyday. But it is as intriguing and freeing as I imagine painters must feel when they realize that they no longer need to name the colors they use. They just paint.

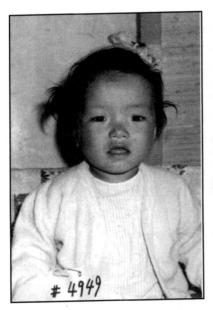

Rebecca Waybill
bwaybill@juno.com

Becky, 36, lives with her family of two cats and a dog. A certified rehabilitation nurse at Ohio State University Hospital, she is a mentor for a freshman nursing student and for her niece. Her new-found passion is gardening and she sees her thumb getting greener every year. Becky feels fortunate to have spent 2 months in Korea during the Olympics.

It Doesn't Get Much Better

Rebecca Waybill

I grew up in a Mennonite family in Scottdale, Pennsylvania with two older brothers and an older sister. From the time I was little, I knew I was adopted. I was always made to feel like a part of the family. I've known no different. Being part of this family obviously molded me into who I am today, including my religious and moral beliefs, my demeanor, and my stubbornness for which I take after my father! They instilled in me the value of family, church and faith in God.

I was teased in grade school because of my features, which was very difficult. From my experience of being teased, my mother wrote a book about me called _Chinese Eyes_. Even though it is classified as fiction, most of it is true. It's about me, being called names and how my mother helped me to see how unimportant it is that some people think I am different.

This book made my sister jealous for a long

time. If I could've looked like other kids back then, believe me, I wouldn't have minded. Through all this, I became more acutely aware of the importance of not treating people differently because of how they looked. After all, who am I to judge someone's appearance? Even today, I hear remarks made about me in passing. It hurts just like it did when I was younger but now I'm not ashamed of my looks. I LIKE how I look.

I am involved in my church community. I have had a chance to speak to couples in my church who are adopting children from China and Central America. They think about their child's names. Should they keep part of their name with their new name? I am very glad to have an all-American name. I may be from Korea but I am an American.

I was very young when I was adopted and have no connections to my birth family or birth country. I'm not ashamed of my background and I tell my story readily but I am who I am because of being in this country and this family. If my Korean name was given by my birth mother, maybe I would feel differently, but she didn't.

I certainly don't have any anger towards my birth mother, but for me, all I remember is America and that my family IS my family. I think it is important that adoptees are told all along that they're adopted and what their situation was before adoption. I would encourage adoptees of all ages to learn about their origins. They should remember that there are special circumstances that put them in the position to be adopted and they need to be open-minded in accepting that part of their life.

Being adopted has given me more opportunity than I could have ever imagined had I stayed in Korea. I don't normally think of myself as adopted but sometimes wonder what it would have been like growing up in Korea or in another family. My parents afforded me a college education and I have had many opportunities that I may never have known in Korea: travel, independence, the joy of being an aunt to seven nieces and nephews, and the ability to buy my own home. It doesn't get much better than that.

Susanne Penner,
<u>smpenner@hotmail.com</u>

Susanne, 28, is a dedicated volunteer to life and is passionate about helping others. In addition to mentoring a 17 year old through Big Brothers/Big Sisters of San Francisco, she also helps a young woman in Nigeria through "Women for Women International." This organization provides women with tools and resources needed to move out of crisis and poverty, and into stability and self-sufficiency. Abandoned at birth with an enlarged liver and spleen due to malnutrition, Susanne was adopted by an Illinois family. Currently, she works in marketing at a computer company.

Beautiful Women

Susanne Penner

When I was about 19, I took my first trip to Korea and it was intimidating. I had a six-foot Caucasian Mormon translator who spoke perfect Korean. We would walk around the shopping areas and the people would ask me questions in Korean (of course) and he would have to answer them. They would giggle. I felt so displaced.

At first I didn't want to leave the hotel. The concierge people were very understanding. They would plan my day-outings and give the driver directions. But on foot, I found myself lost among all these streets that looked the same. Two very kind people helped me find my way back to the hotel. One even left his underground shoe shop to walk me ten blocks to the stairs that led to my hotel.

At that point, I was proud of being Korean. The generosity, warmth and kindness were constant reminders of a part of me that I could relate to. Going back to Korea was daunting on so many levels. When I opened my heart up to it, I felt proud and I felt a sense of belonging. I found what I was looking for.

As I matured, I recognized that I had been touched by a number of wonderful women in my life, the first being my birth mother. In my late 20's, inspired by Mother's Day that was quickly approaching, I wrote the following:

You must have been a beautiful woman the day I was born. Despite your malnutrition and poverty, you must have had beauty and love in your eyes and in your soul. Growing up as a young child, I spoke to you many times in my dreams. Late at night when I wished for you most, you listened. Now I sit here at 28 living in my rented condo in northern California in the United States of America. There is no way you could have imagined this life for me.

I like to think you had mother's intuition. This cannot be the life you dreamed of giving me but I am almost certain that you knew the sacrifice and the true meaning of the word "mother." You gave me physical life. You also gifted me spiritual life that is shared with everyone I meet.

With no record of my birth other than the true fact that I am alive, I am allowed to fantasize about my beginnings. I see you sitting outside of an orphanage in 1973 in a small town near Seoul. I see you smiling at me in a blanket with tears of joy and sorrow running down your face. You leave me outside the orphanage knowing someone will find me shortly soon after you get up and walk away. You were dying inside. Your body was weak but you lived long enough to give me the opportunity of life.

I hope that you have peace in your soul and have a sense of warmth in your heart when you think of me. You gave me a strong spirit and everyone in the orphanage saw that in my eyes. I knew I was loved and cherished by many.

If I had a chance to see you face to face, I would cry at your beauty. I would stare at your face and marvel at the similarities. I would hold your hands in my hands and thank you for my life. I would ask you questions about my birth family, my father, my grandparents and everyone who touched me for the few short weeks we were together. I would tell you about my American family, my boyfriend and my friends. I would share stories of my childhood. I would hold your face in my hands and smile.

Sometimes, when people ask me, "Was it hard growing up and not knowing who your real mother is?" I would answer, "No. Was it hard for you growing up with only one mother?" I was blessed to have many mothers in this lifetime. You gave me life and strong spirit. My foster mother picked me up in the orphanage for my family waiting in the United States. My mom spent the last 27 years raising me with gentle guidance. My stepmother loves my father who is my soulmate, and shares kindness with everyone she meets.

You are among these women who touch all parts of my life. Thank you for being part of this beautiful group of women.

Sunny Jo
midnight.sun@canada.com

Sunny, aka Sonja Sun Young-Joo Park Johnsen, is a 26-year-old Korean adoptee living in Vancouver, Canada. Currently a student majoring in communication, she was adopted to a family in Norway in 1977 at age 1 ½ after being given away by her paternal grandmother without parental approval. She was reunited with her birthparents and sister, Hyo-Jung, in Korea in 2000. In 2001, she also found her older biological brother, Mark, adopted in the USA. Founder of "Kore@n @doptees Worldwide," an online Yahoo! club for Korean adoptees, Sunny has been to Korea four times since 1999.

Confessions of an Adopted Koreweginadian

Sunny Jo

I was adopted in Norway at age one so I could not remember anything about my country of birth. Nor did I have much information about my life before being adopted. I was very interested in Korea and about how I was adopted when I was younger but my parents knew almost nothing about Korea. Few books were available and no Korean people lived nearby. We often talked about adoption and I knew I had a family in Korea. Many times I wondered about them but knew nothing about who they were or why I didn't live with them.

I felt this as an empty spot inside me. My parents told me I used to call "omma" when I was crying as a baby. However, the only parents I knew and could remember were "mamma" and "pappa" so it was natural for us to be a family. They did their very best in raising me with love and care and I had everything I needed. They loved me from the first day.

We grew together as a unity and they always made me feel at home and accepted. What they could not understand, though, was the feeling of being adopted, Korean, and different. They were white and belonged to the mainstream and Norway was their ancestral home.

I love and hate Korea and I also love and hate Norway. All my life I heard about the exceptional Norway, the best country on earth. My parents' ancestors have always lived there and they built this country in one of the world's harshest environments. They lived and died fighting nature; their blood soaked the soil together with sweat and tears.

It makes me proud because I am a Johnsen/ Oislebo as well. I am a full member of this family and I feel the Norwegian soul in myself. Norwegian language is my mother tongue and Norwegian culture is in my fingertips.

But that is only part of the picture. I am not **only** Norwegian, the way my family and friends tried to convince me. I know they hurt when I told them I hated their beloved country, their ancestral home. Norway was all they knew. Norway gave me a new chance. How could I hate it? They didn't understand and they were upset. When I moved abroad, they hoped I would realize that life outside wasn't always better. And they became impatient, told me to settle down and move back home, to stop this stupid obsession of escaping Norway.

Only now, years after my first move abroad,

have they realized that I probably won't move back. They have adjusted to the fact that I will settle a continent away, without being hurt. And now I can return to Norway with pride, embrace my Norwegian culture and love it because I am no longer trapped there.

Norway took my Asian name and culture, told me I should be ashamed of it, and that Norwegian names and habits were better. For years I tried to please them to be accepted in society. But I was never good enough and I could never reach the inner circle of Norway.

Canada. My dream for years, the promised land. I love it unconditionally. I never want to move. It took me years to get there and still years before I can become a citizen. But Canada is mine and I won't give it up. My roots in Canada are fresh. I have no relatives there. So I have to shape my life and my future because my past is somewhere else. My heritage is Korean-Norwegian but my identity is Canadian. Canada accepted me, as I am, never tried to change me. And that's why I love it.

My name is me. Take away my name and you kill the real me. My name has always been of much importance. All I had with me from Korea was my name, Jung Ahn-Sun, the name given to me by the Korean adoption agency. That was me, my only link to my lost past. I kept it as a dear secret as a child. In Norway, I was Sonja Johnsen, named after the Norwegian princess/queen because I was the princess of my parents' lives, their everything. My mother wanted to call me Hanne (Hannah, in English), after her mother, Johanne. But she chose a name more similar to my Korean name. For years, I was only Sonja.

But I started to feel uncomfortable with an all-Norwegian name because I was about to discover my Korean identity. After a long period of emotional preparation I applied for a name-change, Sonja Sun Johnsen at 19. That's when Sunny was born and she did not come out of her shell for a few years. Not before I moved to Canada at the age of 22 was I familiar enough with using Sunny as my main name. Many of my friends don't even know my legal name.

In February 2000, I learned my birth name was Park Young-Joo. It meant little to me because Jung Ahn-Sun was my Korean name. I didn't identify with Young-Joo nor did I know who she was. Two months later I was called that name and I got a déjà vu, a flashback of a feeling from my childhood.

When I first came to Norway, I knew myself as Ahn-Sun but people called me Sonja. I wanted to scream, wanted to protest, but no one understood. I had no power to stop them from taking my name and giving me a new name and identity. When I heard Young-Joo now, I felt exactly the same. NO! Don't take my name. You can't make me into someone I am not! But once again, I was not understood and, once again, I screamed out my frustration, reaching only deaf ears. It would have hurt me less to rip out the heart from my chest.

I still don't feel like Young-Joo nor do I identify with her. But I have come to accept her as one of my hidden identities and maybe one day she'll be ready to leave her shell and come out in public. I did legally change my name once again, to Sonja Sun Young-Joo Johnsen, to acknowledge that she is part of me.

It's only a legality though, known only to my closest friends and family. In practice she rests in my heart, together with Sonja and Ahn-Sun and Pong-ool, a nickname meaning a little bell that was given to me as a baby in Korea. Only Sunny Jo, the Korwegianadian, is awake. And for right now, that is quite enough.

Mark Rodgers
rodgersmd@hotmail.com

Mark, 28, is very excited about his first trip to Korea. He will meet his birth family and relatives for the first time since his adoption at age 3. He was reunited with his birth sister, Sunny Jo, to his right in the picture. To his left is his other birth sister, Hyo-Jung. "Letters...." is a collection of recent correspondence with his birth family. Mark works for General Motors as a supplier manager.

Letters....

Mark Rodgers

Dear Korean parents,

My name is Mark Rodgers and I am your Korean son – In Kwon. I was notified by my adoption agency here in the U.S. about 2 months ago that I had Korean birth parents looking for me. I was very shocked when I heard of this because my adoptive parents and I were told that I had no surviving relatives in Korea.

About a month later, I was informed of Sunny's email address by the adoption agency. I was soon able to locate her website which details her accounts of her visits to Korea and meeting you and the rest of the Korean family. Since then, I've been in touch with Sunny by phone and email and we are currently communicating.

She has been very helpful in providing me with many answers to questions that I've had regarding my past. I've seen the videos of her reunion with our Korean family as well as her parents in Norway. It was very exciting and shocking.

I graduated from high school in 1991 and went on to college and graduated from Wayne State University in 1999 with a bachelor's degree in Business Marketing and Management. I currently work at General Motors Corporation and my title is "Buyer." I purchase and provide business for automotive suppliers with General Motors. I am responsible for over $200 million dollars worth of business. I can tell you more about my job later.

Some of my favorite activities and hobbies include playing baseball, tennis, basketball, camping, hiking, fishing, automobiles, and hanging out with my friends. I currently live in an apartment with my younger brother in a city that is about 40 minutes west of Detroit, Michigan.

I have a loving family that includes my Mother, Father, and younger brother, also adopted from Korea. My family has two dogs, Rascal and Shelby. I have many aunts, uncles and cousins from both my parents' side. I have Grandparents from my Father's side that live in the northern part of Michigan. Everyone in my immediate family has graduated from college. My father is an accountant, my mother a home-maker and a substitute teacher, and my brother an elementary school teacher.

I am very proud of my family and everything that they have given me. I would not be the man I am now if it were not for them. I feel that my life is where I had always hoped that it would be. I am beginning to settle into my life with confidence and security. My career is on an exciting and rewarding path, I have a great relationship with my family, and I have very good and close friends.

After I've learned that I have a younger sister, Sunny, who went through the trials of adoption like I did, my goal was to get to know her (after 23 years) and be her "big brother." I also learned of another younger sister and I hope that we will also be able to get to know each other.

I do not know what will come from our relationship, but I'd like to hear your stories and know your feelings about my abandonment in Korea 23 years ago. Sunny has told me her story and what you have shared with her but I need to know from you what really happened and why it took 23 years to find me.

I'm willing to keep the channel of communication open and I'll listen with an open mind and heart but please understand that I've grown up to be a responsible adult in America and I'm no longer a lost child.

I hope that someday we may be able to move past everything that has happened in our past and I hope that we can all find the peace and love within ourselves that I think we all deserve.

Sincerely,

Mark

Dear In Kwon,

In Kwon! How long I've wanted to call this name in person.....

It's been already 25 years that we were apart from each other. I'm wondering if you remember that we visited your grandparents on your mother's side by train. They ran a restaurant at that time and your grandmother, you, Sunny, your uncles, and your aunt all lived together. There was a well in our backyard and there was a small store outside of our house. I can remember all the details of the moments we were together. You loved a wooden horse very much and liked to play with it. You were called "Doma" (Thomas in Korean).

From now on I'll tell you what happened in the past. Your father and I fell in love and got married young – I was 20 and your father was 21. At that time, your grandmother lived in Cheju Island and I lived with her there. Though things have changed a lot, it was a must at that time when a woman got married, she had to live with her parents-in-law. We were all happy in the beginning but after your father left us to serve in the army, things got tough.

Your father used to be a breadwinner of our family. But, your grandmother had to support all of the family members and you and I were a heavy burden on her. She hated it and kicked us out of her house. She moved to Anyang with the rest of her family and did not even tell us where they had moved. After a while I tried my best to find them because I wanted to hear news from your father. She told me lies that your father did not love me any more and intercepted all of his letters to me. She even told your father that I left him for a new life.

Your father went on leave to find you and me. No one knew that it'd be the very beginning of a tragedy. In such a short vacation time your father went everywhere to find me and at last found me on the last day of his leave. It was too late for him to be back to the barrack, though. He ran away from the police, and you and I had to be with your grandmother.

Everyday, policemen came to her house and gave us hard time to find your father. Your grandmother did not tolerate it and kicked me out of her house again and abandoned you and Sunny (Young-Joo). After I found out that she did that, I visited every orphanage all over the place. No one in the family told me where she abandoned you. I never even considered that you could've been adopted abroad, outside of Korea, because they told me that you were adopted by a certain principal of a high school. After I found Sunny, I wondered if you were adopted abroad, outside of Korea. It was all Sunny's effort to find you.

I hope this may answer your questions – though roughly. Please ask anything you want to know. I'll answer it with all the truth. I've been always sad, as I did not even know whether you were alive or dead. And now, I feel better as I now know at least that you've become a respectable adult. I hope that we can forget the bitter memories in the past and forgive. I'm also attaching the certification of your baptism – a week after your birth.

Please take good care. Love always, Mom

Dear Parents,

I received your letter and ours is a story of tragedy and sorrow as well as thankfulness and celebration.

As I have discovered through you and Sunny, I was given away for adoption without your consent or knowledge. Because of a hateful grandmother and cultural influences, we've been robbed 25 years of our lives from ever knowing each other. Tragically, we'll never be able to recapture those lost years. I could easily become consumed by rage and depression if I only focused on the injustices that fell upon me 25 years ago.

As I try and make sense of all that has happened, I've begun to realize that many wonderful things have happened from the result of my adoption. I would never have known the wonderful parents who raised and loved me as well as my brother and all of my adopted family members. I never would have known the close and wonderful friends that I've made throughout my life and I never would have had all of the opportunities that I've been blessed with.

It has been my past experiences and those people in it who have helped me develop into the man that I have now become. I am proud of who I am and of all the things that I have accomplished in my life thus far.

In a strange twist of fate, destiny has given

me an opportunity to regain a heritage that I once lost many years ago. It has allowed me to learn of a Korean family that I never knew I had. More importantly, it has allowed me to finally discover the story of my adoption.

I'm still trying to work out many issues in my mind but I only ask that you remain patient with me. Meanwhile, we can continue to write letters so that we can further understand each other.

Yours truly,

Mark

Dear Mark's Parents:

I am writing this letter to you to say "thank you" for raising Mark for all these years. My name is Jin-Sun, Mark's birth father. I was born in 1952 and now have a small business.

It's been already 23 years since we lost In Kwon. We never thought that he was adopted overseas and looked for him only in Korea. In the 70's, Korea was a very poor country. The economy was in quite a bad condition and people were just poor and helpless. I had to go to the army (it is a must here) when Mark was 3. My mother's distorted decision made us separate from each other. It is no use to tell now who was to blame for the misfortune. It was such a painful experience that we can never forget it. Only our will that we should find Mark and Sunny someday made us strong-minded and continue looking for the abandoned children.

I cannot thank you enough for raising Mark. I believe that God led him to such good parents. I will pray for you and Mark for the rest of my life. Not a single day has passed without praying for Mark. I cannot express my gratitude to you enough in words. I feel ashamed of myself for not being able to protect my children.

Best regards,

JS

Appendix

Resources for Adopted Koreans

Adopted Korean - Chicago
www.koreanadoptees.org
Network for Chicago Korean adoptees

Adopterade Koreaners Forening
www.akf.nu
Network for Swedish adopted Koreans

AKConnection (AdoptedKoreanConnection)
www.akconnection.com/
Network for Minnesota Korean adoptees

Also-Known-As, Inc. (AKA)
www.alsoknownas.org/home.tpl
Network for New York Korean adoptees

Also-Known-As, Inc., D.C. Chapter
www.washington.alsoknownas.org/
Network for Washington Korean adoptees

Arierang
www.arierang.nl
Network for Dutch Korean adoptees

Asian Adult Adoptees of Washington (AAAW)
www.aaawashington.org/
Network for Washington Asian adoptees

Association of Korean Adoptees – San Francisco (AKA-SF)
www.geocities.com/tokyo/garden/3947/
Network for San Francisco Korean adoptees

Dongari Switzerland
www.dongari.ch/
Network for Swiss Korean adoptees

The Evan B. Donaldson Adoption Institute
www.adoptioninstitute.org/
Research, policy and practice information about adoption

First Person Plural
www.pbs.org/pov/firstpersonplural/index.html
Educational resource based on Deann Borshay Liem's film, First Person Plural

Global Overseas Adoptees' Link (G.O.A.L)
www.goal.or.kr
Network for Overseas Adopted Koreans (OAKs) living and working in Korea

Kimchi Club
www.geocities.com/kimchi_club/
Network for Australian adopted Koreans in Canberra

Kore@n @doptees Worldwide
http://groups.yahoo.com/group/koreanadopteesworldwide/
Network for worldwide Korean adoptees

Korean-American Adoptee/Adoptive Family Network (KAAN)
www.KAANet.com
Information and resources related to Korean adoption

Third International Gathering of Adult Adoptees
www.adopteegathering.org
Information about the Third International Gathering of Adult Adoptees in August, 2003, in Seoul, Korea

National Organizations

Inter-National Adoption Alliance (IAA)
www.i-a-a.org
Resources for adoptees and adoptive families with information on waiting children worldwide

Joint Council on International Children's Services (JCICS)
www.jcics.org/
Intercountry adoption agencies promoting ethical practice and child welfare services

North American Council on Adoptable Children (NACAC)
www.nacac.org
Adoptive family support, education and information

Adoption and Adoptive Parenting Information and Resources

Adopted Child
www.raisingadoptedchildren.com
Educational material for adoptive parenting

International Concerns Committee for Children
www.iccadopt.org
Resource for families on international adoption

National Adoption Information Clearinghouse
www.calib.com/naic
Summaries of state by state law, databases of agencies, support groups, information for families beginning the adoption process

Office of Children's Issues (International Adoptions), U.S. Department of State
www.travel.state.gov/adopt.html
International adoption laws; INS requirements and processes

Rainbow Kids
www.Rainbowkids.com
International adoption process, agencies and waiting child listenings

The Welcome Garden
www.welcomegarden.com
Agency and waiting child listings

Resources for Cultural Books and Items; Adoption-related Books, Videos, Publications and Software

Asia for Kids
www.asiaforkids.com

Celebrate the Child
www.celebratechild.com

Cultural Keepsakes
www.culturalkeepsakes.org

Korean Quarterly
www.koreanquarterly.org
Publication promoting Korean American issues and culture

Perspectives Press
www.perspectivespress.com

Tapestry Books
www.tapestrybooks.com

Yeong and Yeong Book Company
www.yeongandyeong.com/

Newsletters and Magazines

Adoptive Families Magazine
www.AdoptiveFamiliesMagazine.com
National magazine for pre and post adoptive families

Adoption Medical News
www.adoptionmedicalnews.com
Information on adoption and health

Adoption Today International
www.adoptinfo.net
Articles on adoption issues

Raising Adopted Child
www.raisingadoptedchildren.com
Resource for raising adopted children

186

About the Editors

Sook Wilkinson, Ph.D. is the author of **Birth is More than Once: The Inner World of Adopted Korean Children**. As a clinical psychologist in Bloomfield Hills, Michigan, and at the Center for Human Development, William Beaumont Hospital, she has devoted her career to working with internationally adopted children and their families. As a woman born and educated through college in Korea, she offers an invaluable perspective on international adoption. She is a frequent presenter at professional and adoption conferences on cross-cultural issues, parenting and various aspects of international adoption. With her husband, Todd, they are the proud parents of TJ and Gina.

Nancy Fox is one of the founders and Executive Director of Americans for International Aid and Adoption established in 1975. She is a national and international speaker on adoption and child welfare. Recipient of the "Friend of Children" award from North American Council on Adoptable Children, she has served on the Board and been past president of Joint Council on International Children's Services. She and her husband, Jon, are parents of seven children, "home-grown" and internationally adopted.

187

Courtesy Order Form

Please send me _____ copies of *After the MORNING CALM: Reflections of Korean Adoptees* at $16.95 each.

$_____

Please send me _____ copies of *Birth is More than Once: The Inner World of Adopted Korean Children* at $12.95 each. $_____

MI residents, please add 6% tax $_____

Shipping in US $4.50 for the first copy. Please add $0.50 for each additional copy. $_____

On orders of 10-20, discount 10%* $_____

Total Amount Due $_____

* For larger order, please contact us.

Payment in U.S. funds must accompany order. Please make check payable and send orders to:
Sunrise Ventures
SunriseVentures@hotmail.com
708 Parkman Dr. Bloomfield Hills, MI 48304

Name_____
Please print legibly.

Address_____

City _____State _____ Zip _____

Unconditional Money Back Guarantee. If you find the book unsuitable for any reason, please return it for a full refund minus the shipping cost.

A portion of the proceeds from the book will be donated to a charitable project.

Also available from Sunrise Ventures

Birth is More than Once:
The Inner World of Adopted Korean Children

Hei Sook Park Wilkinson, Ph.D.

Do you ever wonder why some adopted Korean children shun other Koreans, hoard things, or tend to overeat? This research based book will help you understand their inner world. Learn why being teased can become a crisis. Share their fantasies about their birth parents.
73 pages, $12.95